THE WRITING LESSON

THE WRITING LESSON

Linda Lanterman

This book is a work of fiction. All characters in this book are fictitious, and any resemblance to actual persons, living or dead, is purely coincidental.

ISBN: 0-75960-439-8

This book is printed on acid free paper.

1stBooks – rev. 11/14/00

For Aldora and Mrs. DeHas

Special thanks to Wallis Leslie, Livvy Coupe and Mary Rosseau who read and edited several drafts. Thanks to the Lake of the Pines Book Club who took <u>The Writing Lesson</u> as a Selection of the Month and provided invaluable feedback. Thanks also to the Los Altos Tennis and Philosophy group, Jane Stefani, Jan Edwards, Judy Mutch and Marilyn Shodiss for their friendship, encouragement and assistance. Summer writing workshops at Foothill College and the writers' group established by JoAnn Daugherty, Sandy Saidak, Anatole Wilson and Vicky Mlyniec provided critiques and inspiration. To my husband, Douglas, and to my family, I am indebted for their patience and support. I also owe thanks to the University of Georgia, Athens, to Pat Byrd DeMeester and my sisters at the Beta Sigma chapter of Alpha Chi Omega, and to my other alma mater, the University of California, Berkeley. "Let There Be Light."

Linda Lanterman

1.

Doctor's pushing me to get help. "Call a friend," he says. The ankle will cause the most trouble. Red mud splatters from this rural suburb of Atlanta cover my tan slacks, slit past the knee. The doctor's slapping on wet plaster strips and talking about a walking cast after some weeks. His voice bounces off me in the harsh light of the examining room. "There has to be someone you can call," he says. But there isn't. The nurse pushes a name and number in front of me, hands me the phone.

How has it happened that I have come this far with so few true friends? You'll tell me it has to do with trust and my fear of trust betrayed. You'd be right. I didn't start out to live a lie, but once I started spinning sticky webs I became caught fast as any prey. There's only Susan.

Susan Ladona is a cherished friend, but a long distance one I've seen just twice in twenty years. We write letters, occasionally phone. Susan and I don't talk about that summer we met, in the writing class, in 1958. I was doing graduate work.

She was an early entry freshman. It was a tough summer for her. Anyway, she didn't kill the professor. Just watched him depart, so to speak.

"Mrs. Henrietta Elmers? This is Vivian Titch. My doctor recommended you. Dr. Swain. I'm calling from his office. Going to be needing help for at least eight weeks, he says."

"Must've broken something then."

"Right ankle and my left wrist."

"Lordy. How'd you do that?"

"Well, I, I was wading in the creek, if you must know."

"Creek? Down here we say branch."

I'm trying to understand the tone. Is this someone I want taking care of me? I'd like some sympathy and I'm not hearing any.

"Of course, if you're busy --"

"Where do you live? Any pets? Can't abide furry things in the house. Dog or cat hair rolling along the floor, everywhere, getting into the food."

I cover the phone, turn to the nurse and mouth, "There's got to be someone else." She waves me off with a pooh pooh smile and mouths back, "She's the best."

"Ah, no pets. I don't have a pet." I'd been thinking of getting a calm dog or cat from the pound, though, for company. Maybe I live too far out of town.

"Do you drive, Henrietta? I live at the end of Plumnelly Road. I've rented the Tyler place, little brick house with a screened porch, creek runs along one side down to the pond."

"Describes most houses in town. Car's not reliable, but I drive. Bus'd be better. Need to charge you for gas or bus fare, either way."

"Well, of course. . . " I frown. Who is this woman? The nurse told me she was an elderly black woman, strong, serious, with lots of heart. I don't hear any heart.

"Can't abide another old fussbudget like the last one Dr. Swain sent my way," she says. "How old are you?"

"Forty-tw-- What does that have to do with . . .? Why, how old are you?"

"Humph. We'll get along just fine, Mrs. Titch. You tell Dr. Swain my hourly rate's a dollar higher than he's been telling his patients. He ought to write it down this time. He keeps forgettin'. You need me this evening? Or not 'til morning?"

The conversation isn't going the way I might have imagined. Maybe its shock. The shock of the fall.

"How you getting home from the doctor's office?"

"A neighbor. My neighbor's here with me. She'll bring me home and settle me in for the night. But she works."

"Look for me at eight in the morning, then."

5

"Don't worry," says the nurse, with a grin that shows too many teeth. "Sounds like it's settled."

No one understands. I frown at the solicitous nurse helping me into my neighbor's car and pretend I'm in too much pain to remember to thank her.

Home, in bed, I think of ways to fend for myself. I like my privacy. I don't need that much assistance. Some shopping, making up the bed. I wiggle my fingers to prove to myself it's just a crack, a hairline of a break in one little bone in my wrist. Another matter, the ankle, but I can hop. I'll make do with spit baths and TV dinners. Sometime before dawn, I realize I'm being silly. Just when I'm trying to reclaim my life, I have to admit I need help.

Earlier than I'd like, my neighbor brings coffee and cornmeal muffins and helps me navigate with a chair as a makeshift walker. She'll be gone ten days, she says. An overnight development? To visit her mother in Augusta. She lets me know with gracious determination that it's her Christian duty to befriend her new neighbor, but I shouldn't count on too much. I thank her with superlatives. Relief in her every gesture, I notice, when I tell her the woman I called from the doctor's office will work out, I'm sure. I don't have the exact accent, but I know the patterned nuances of the form. If friendship with this neighbor is out there, it's dangling beyond my vision.

At eight ten, Henrietta knocks and I call to her to come in.

"Mornin'. Bus ran late." She's a large woman, frizzy grey hair, a bit wild. A tall, black woman whose demeanor is larger still. And the chin! That jutting chin. And eyes that could warn off the Devil. I know that face, that stance, the sloping shoulders, the tilt of the head.

"Henrietta! Oh, my God! It's you, Henrietta."

She regards me with interested disdain. The eyes blink, focus harder, two fingers scratch at her jawbone, under her ear. "I don't do psychiatric cases."

"The sorority house, at William and Mary, a hundred years ago," I say in typical exaggeration. Her expression doesn't change, but the eyes soften.

"The girl from California?" she asks. I nod and she remembers. "Vivian. Yes. Didn't used to wear glasses. Titch isn't right. The rich Atlanta family?"

"My married name. I don't remember your last name either," I say, not sure I ever knew it.

"Chance, before I married, Elmers, then Covell after. When my second husband died, I went back to Elmers. Plain ol' Henrietta is fine." The warmth left her eyes when she said Covell, but creeps back. Perhaps it's my imagination.

She had been the cook at the sorority house for thirty-two years and I know she can give as good as she gets from white folks. I don't know how old she is. Must be pushing seventy. It's not the kind of thing you ask Henrietta, I laugh to myself, recalling yesterday's phone call. What, I wonder, did she hear in my tone during that conversation?

I met Henrietta when I was a freshman in college in Williamsburg, Virginia, seven years before I met Susan. Henrietta is a friend. At least someone who knows who I once was. A possible friend. My delight at seeing her again is tempered by her cool demeanor. I want us to become friends, respectful friends, but there's a distance.

She says she remembers me. Maybe she does, but I wasn't the only sister to come from California. There had to be a few others over the years. I remember her. Best cook on campus, but Henrietta ruled her kitchen, and the sisters, through fear, and she applied as much "finishing" to us as Mother Cee did at her awful formal dinners each month. We had to attend those monthly dinners in ball gowns and watch our manners. Henrietta taught us manners too.

I always liked Henrietta, liked her no-nonsense dignity, but I never directly experienced her wrath. Henrietta didn't allow sass, and occasionally, she would have to remind a young woman of that. She must live in many memories, one way or the other.

Surreptitiously, while we talk, she eyes the cardboard box of books on the floor by the bookcase.

"Doctor's office said your husband died last month. I'm sorry." She pauses, moves to the box. Why has she been talking to the doctor's office, I wonder.

"You've read all these?" Creased fingers reach to touch, then lift the books on top to see others." Reverence in her hands, if not her face.

"I ran out of space on the shelves. I have everything else unpacked, pretty much. House is more settled than my life."

"We'll find places for them," she says. "Every room should have some."

"Good. I leave that to you."

She carries her purse and large paper sack to the kitchen and returns in a white bib apron. "Good gracious! What's the matter with those toes?" She leans over the footstool where my ankle is propped. "Lordy, they're purple! Can you move them?"

"Aches like hell, if you must know. The heat, I guess." My hand reaches out to try to stop her from manipulating them. She disappears and comes back with three pillows, raises my ankle higher.

"You got that doctor's number handy?" Disappears again.

She calls. Bits of an indignant conversation reach me in the living room. She returns with her purse, apron still in place. "I'll need your keys. We're going in."

On the way, Henrietta's driving makes me forget about my swollen toes. She was right to take the bus, but I don't make a peep of criticism. Maybe she's not used to my car.

At the office, Henrietta and Dr. Swain confer over my ankle like I'm a horse they might have to shoot. Must not have kept it elevated enough, they decide. I'm not going to argue. Hot, purple toes keep me quiet. The doctor slits the cast down one side with his circular saw, straps it so it won't expand too much, and gives Henrietta more instructions than she needs to hear. "Uh huh. Uh huh." She nods to the doctor and glances at me. I wink back. Her face is blank, unreadable.

She stuffs me into the back seat of the car, my ankle up on pillows and drives to her house. She's going to pack a suitcase. I need round the clock care, she says.

I do not! I'm tired and crabby, that's all. Treating me like a two year old. She stops the car and goes up sagging wooden steps to a small frame house with a rusty tin roof and no paint, except around the window frames. An old pecan tree shades a small, swept dirt yard, white and purple cosmos bloom along the walk. A rocker with a flat, stringy cushion and a wooden armchair decorate the porch. A couple of people amble by, covertly curious.

I wait, stuck in the car's back seat. An elderly man, crippled by arthritis, goes up the steps to carry Henrietta's suitcase. She gives him the honor of helping her and introduces him to me. He looks in the open car door at the white woman in plaster. A good man, kind eyes.

At my house we settle into a routine, Henrietta's routine, and although I like the company and need the help, I start counting the days until the casts come off. Henrietta asked if she could read some of my books. Says she's never read anything by Susan Ladona, but she's heard of her.

"Writes childrens' books, doesn't she?"

"Well, they classified her first books as young adult. Probably because her main characters were young people, teens. But I never felt the classification was quite right. They have deeper, darker elements to them. Especially after the first two."

"Kinda like Tom Sawyer and Huck Finn?"

Henrietta doesn't see my wide-eyed stare. She's studying the bookcase. "Ah, yes, kind of like Twain. She really broke into the mainstream with <u>Clog Dancer</u>. Her protagonist is a young woman, but the story's about both the value and the suffocating oppression of cultural traditions. Wonderful book. Good place to start. That one, or <u>Death at Big Muddy</u>."

"Believe I'd like to start with her first one. For the progression, the development."

"You plan to read them all? What if you don't like her?"

"Think I will. <u>The Atlanta Journal</u> carried an article about her some years back. Sunday book section. I'll give her a fair try."

Henrietta is a fast reader. When she starts her second Ladona book, I ask how she likes Susan's writing. Lots of other authors to choose from. She looks at me like it's a trick question. "Did you like the story? That's all I'm asking."

"Lots of bugs."

"Bugs?"

"Yeah, and snakes and swamp things. Good story, though. That little Jenny was something. And it was interesting to learn what roots and plants you can eat."

"Susan lives in New York now, but she was raised in Waycross."

"It sure enough shows." Henrietta turns back a couple of pages. "Listen to how this one starts: 'Every evening Unk polishes the thick glass of the eight cubicles in his snake house. It's his special time with them. He checks on each snake with this ritual. Even when I help him, he'll swipe his rag over the glass of the ones I've done, but he isn't looking for fingerprints. He's watching the snakes. Daddy taught me about snakes, but Unk taught me more. He knew that I was the one who shared his feelings for them. Everybody's interested, but what I mean is, Unk and I understand them. He taught me to think like a snake.'"

I hear the fluid animation in her voice. She leans back in her chair. A pinpoint of light sparkles in each eye even as she glowers at me. "You have to wonder what kind of child thinks like a snake."

"That character is based on a life Susan knew. Her uncle has a snake house at his alligator farm." I pause.

"Want to know her story?" I ask, casting a baited line I'll draw in slowly, hoping for a nibble. "I could tell you a bit of it each evening after supper."

Her chin goes higher. Her finger runs along a scar on the side of her face. She's watching. Is it genuine interest in Susan, or is she humoring me?

Linda Lanterman

2.

"Suppose I do wonder what kind of woman admits she thinks like a snake. You could tell me about Susan Ladona tomorrow evening," Henrietta says. "After I finish the dishes."

In the middle of the night, my conscience comes calling. Wants to chat. Over and over I battle myself. I've never revealed Susan's story. Why now? I don't have to tell every detail. I mean, it wasn't murder. But some prosecutor would have tried to charge murder or at least manslaughter, I'm sure. Susan had motive. Henrietta might not be that interested, but I think she is. Conscience retreats. I begin to weave the beginning. I'll figure out what to do with the end later. The next evening my conscience returns, and after the dishes, we read. Well, Henrietta reads, and I pretend to.

I didn't tell her Susan's story that night, or the one after that. Henrietta hasn't said anything more, so I've skipped it and let a couple of weeks drift by. Sleep is coming harder, though. Susan's story circles in my dreams, bangs on the walls of my mind.

Tuesday, instead of "Morning, Miss Vivian," I get, "You look terrible. Bad night?"

"Hard to sleep in this heavy thing. My ankle's been bothering me."

"Uh huh. Looks okay to me."

"Can I have some coffee, please?"

Henrietta commandeered a real walker for me. Doesn't tell me where. It has an apparatus for my forearm so I don't put too much weight on my wrist. She has an admirable way of cutting through the medical establishment and getting results. I navigate around the kitchen to my chair with the walker's punctuated motions. I sit. She puts a mug in front of me, then pours from a three foot elevation. Not a drop touches the table cloth.

"Bet you can't do that with a tea cup," I say, trying not to be intimidated.

"Hush now. After breakfast you can shell those peas, if you want to help out, like you said yesterday."

The paper sack is opposite my plate of scrambled eggs and grits. "Okay. May I have some more juice, please?"

She picks up the glass and pours juice from the pitcher in the normal way. We're back on track.

Henrietta and I are learning to trust each other, maybe. I depend on her. She likes my books, at least. She's going through my whole collection.

After supper each evening, we sit on the screened porch of this little house on the edge of a mud red pond, watch the fireflies, read, and share stories, other stories. I don't get quite as weepy as I did when I arrived. Henrietta has been widowed twice. She has a married son who teaches agronomy at the University in Athens, and a daughter in Atlanta, but her grandchildren have moved to Trenton, Des Moines, and Jacksonville. In her stoic way, she comforts me. I learn from her every day. I can be sad, but I can't mope, Henrietta has told me. She won't have it.

She knows more about me than I know about her. She always had a sense of mystery. Nothing you can say exactly, a hidden thing. It's there when she's upset or watching something on the news. Her finger will trace the long, almost invisible scar from under her chin around to the front of her right ear. She had the scar when I was in college, but I'd forgotten it. I've asked her about it. She said she might tell me one day.

I think she knows I'll probably leave when my hurt recedes, that I'm here just a few months. That's what I told her, but I doubt I'll return to Atlanta. I have no family in California and none I care about in Atlanta. I don't know where I'll go. Maybe Henrietta knows more about that than I do.

Henrietta and I still talk of our surprise at finding each other, after all this time, and in Georgia, not Virginia. She believes in signs, messages from God, she calls them. "Foolishness," I said, but I'm starting to wonder. Henrietta and Susan always have believed. The problem with signs is reading them correctly.

I awake early and start breakfast as quietly as I can. A simple breakfast to surprise Henrietta. But she's not happy. At the kitchen door her head jerks, surveying the scene and me at the stove pouring rolled oats from the box into the pot.

"What you doing up so early? Thought we had burglars. Better get off that ankle."

"I wanted to fix breakfast so you could rest."

"How could I rest with all that noise? What you pay me for?"

I sit. Henrietta inspects the pot on the stove. "What's this? Mush! You must have used a whole box of raisins. We going to eat this with a knife and fork? Look at this mess. So stiff you can't stir it. So many fat raisins, you'll be passing gas the whole day long!"

"You said you liked raisins."

"In the proper amount. You used the whole box. You did. You used the whole box. Not a sprinkling. No, you used the whole box. The spoon stands straight up in this mess. You call this oatmeal? It's a rock."

"Didn't use the whole box."

"You're sure no cook."

"I like it stiff with lots of raisins. That's all. Sort of like eating cookies. I only wanted to help."

"Don't you like the way I cook?" Her arms fold across her chest. I hear her breathing in and out. Heat creeps up my face. I bite my index finger to stop my lip from trembling.

"Henrietta, you're a wonderful cook. Please don't . . ."

"Well, if this is how you like your mush, you can have it. I'm fixing me some eggs." She dumps the glob into a small stainless mixing bowl and puts it in front of me. Then the milk carton and a box of brown sugar, not the pitcher or the sugar bowl. "You're going to need these for your 'cookies'."

My appetite's gone. Henrietta leaves me at the kitchen table, scrambles two eggs, scrapes them onto a plate and takes her breakfast out the back door to the porch. I'm rethinking how much I really need this kind of help.

On her way back inside, she stops in the doorway and waits, shifting her weight until I notice her.

"I'm sorry, Miss Vivian, but you hurt my feelings.

"You hurt mine, too. I wanted to be useful, that's all."

"Don't like folks cookin' in my kitchen."

It's heating up again. I hear it in our voices. I apologize without much conviction, stand and slide the mixing bowl with the partially eaten oatmeal toward the sink.

"I'll be fixing potato salad and roast beef sandwiches for lunch, but I could make peanut butter and sugar, like cookies, if you want," says Henrietta as I leave the room.

"Henrietta, let's not do this."

"You hurt my feelings."

"You hurt mine too. I'm sorry," I say, but I still leave the room and recount the days until my cast comes off. The morning is shot.

Afternoon thunder showers add to the gloom. Cautiously I stick my head into the kitchen. Henrietta is working on a loaf of bread, cutting it length-wise, twice. I sit and watch in silence, fascinated. She spreads one long slice with flavored, thinned, creamed cheese, another with seasoned mustard, another with seasoned mayonnaise and the last with a thick sauce I can't identify. She uses a hint of chopped olive, pickle, very thin slices of ham, cheese, a sprinkling of shredded lettuce and bit of red cabbage, very finely cut, just for color. On the other layer go thin roast beef strips, a light brushing of horseradish in sour cream. When at last all is assembled, she returns to the bowl of softened cream cheese and 'frosts' the entire loaf, even piping along the top edges and decorating it with pimento strip flowers.

"Wow!" I say.

Henrietta permits herself a small smile.

"A work of art."

"It's for dinner tomorrow. Let the flavors blend overnight," she says. I remind myself that 'dinner' means lunch, although once in a while Henrietta uses the word lunch.

"I've never seen anything like it!"

"Before I serve it, I'll put three egg slices here." While she carefully wraps the loaf, she says, "Visiting nurse is coming tomorrow. In case she decides to come at dinner time, we'll be ready."

Susan's new book arrives from New York today and I tear into package. Forgetting myself, and the visiting nurse, I read the inscription and hug the book to my body. The dedication surprises me when I see my name in print: Dedicated to Vivian Titch and to the memory of Lucrecia Barry. Then there's her usual note in green ink, To Vivian, Loyally in the bond of friendship, Susan. She knows without talking to me that I will consider the dedication a mistake, perhaps her only mistake in all this time. She also knows it's unnecessary to make this gesture of thanks, but she's gone and done it, as they say. I imagine her with the fountain pen she uses while picking up the first bound copy, turning to the flyleaf. I can see her uncapping her pen and writing the note in her precise lettering.

This time there's an extra note on a folded sheet of white stationery. It slid to my lap when I opened the book. The insistent, buzz-fly nurse begins fussing about, making excited noises. If the story is anything like the truth -- Too late, I try refusing to acknowledge my friendship with the author.

"There must be hundreds of Vivian Titches in this country and the United Kingdom."

Nurse Martha frowns. "But it's an advance copy. The book stores don't have this one yet. Of course, you're the one. Titch is not a common name. You have all her books. All signed. Don't be so modest. Tell me about her. Please."

"What you doin' going through my stuff. How you know I have all her books? Henrietta! Henrietta!"

But Martha is insistent. "Hush you now, Miss Vivian. I'm on to you. Stop swinging your hands around like that or you'll break your other arm."

"Henrietta! There you are! Tell this nurse we don't need her a minute longer and show her to the door!"

Henrietta shuffles into view, stopping in the doorway, slowing the tempo. "She knows where the door is," she says. Hearing her pronounce <u>door</u> like <u>dough</u>, I almost laugh, but she's still talking in my direction and I don't dare. "I told you it was plum foolish to have some ol' county people come in here. We fine. But no. You had to call the visitin' nurses jus' cause some quack doctor thinks it might be a good idea."

Martha recoils. "Quit oozing southern on me you two. I've seen your act. It might work on some, but I know you're both educated, and Henrietta's a Yankee, besides.

"As for you, Miss Vivian, that silly business may work on your doctor, but you've never fooled me. I'll forget the Ladona book, since it upsets you, but I expect you to be honest and straightforward with me."

Her sincerity makes me contrite, and troubled. Nurse Martha turns to frown at Henrietta too. Henrietta looks the woman up and down, as if measuring her for a fight.

Why have I overreacted? "I apologize, Martha. Susan Ladona and I were in the same writing class in college one summer."

"I knew it." Martha smiles in triumph.

"We became friends, but I'm most reluctant to have anyone know about our friendship. People always want to take advantage of celebrity connections." Martha's smile vanishes with a solemn shake of her head.

"You wouldn't, I know, but if you told people, someone would want me to have her do a charity function, say, for a new hospital wing or for abused children or a thousand other wonderful causes. Think how bad it would make me feel when she turned me down on each one of them. People would believe I didn't really know her after all. They'd become angry with me, and Susan too, by extension."

"Was it at the University of Georgia? There must be lots of people who remember her."

"It was in California, Martha. Not in Georgia." I consider whether Martha will accept this. The nurse knows I'm from California, by way of Williamsburg and Atlanta. I've kept my voice even, unchanged, I hope, and look the nurse in the eye, the way I used to lie when I needed to. Henrietta leans on the door frame behind Martha and watches me with dark disapproval, rich mocha arms folded across her breasts. She's always known a lie when she heard one.

Martha steps back to see us both at the same time, Henrietta in the doorway and me sitting in one of the overstuffed wing chairs with the hard cast surrounding my broken ankle propped on the ottoman, and my arm strapped in a lightweight, removable cast. Henrietta transfers her glare to Martha in time for the nurse to think she'd been its object all along. Martha moves forward, picks up the novel from the carpet where it had slipped in my futile tantrum and places it in my lap.

"Your secret's safe. I didn't mean to upset you. Just making conversation. I'll be checking on you one last time next Wednesday, if you want me to."

"That'll be fine, Martha. It'll be nice to see you."

"Mo' iced tea, Miss Martha?" Henrietta is getting even, her price for joining me in the act. The ritual plays itself out, Nurse Martha politely declining and thanking us for lunch and saying her good-byes.

Henrietta closes the door and sticks her head into the living room. "That interview you wanted to hear will be on in 'bout twenty minutes. I got some baking to finish."

"Nurse Martha certainly liked the sandwich loaf. Three helpings," I say as Henrietta heads for the kitchen. Her head turned for an instant, and I thought I saw a smile.

In my lap, Susan's note is folded in thirds. I unfold it with my good hand.

Vivian, You will recognize many things in this book, my eighth. I had to write about that summer. I finally pulled out the memories, held them to the light and braided a novel from them.

Twenty-two years ago, I wrote the first draft of this novel, not the way Hamilton Jestin would have liked, but the way it happened. Beat it out on my old Royal portable, the one I had at school, with the round, sticking keys constantly interrupting. No Picnic was the title before the publisher changed it. I

25

still have the original title page, ripped from a spiral notebook. Smeared the words on the paper with my index finger, dipped in his blood.

That sheet of paper has rested on top of the first draft all this time, hidden where no one will find it. One day I'll burn it, or feed it to an alligator. There will be a sign. I had to write about that summer -- to clear the way for the sign.

Yes, I'll recognize it. I will know. -- Susan

Has she really done it? I flutter the pages of the slim novel. The sound of tired footsteps arouse me from my thoughts and I look up to see Henrietta lumber into the room. Sloping shoulders and big feet. She holds her head high and slightly to one side, her chin out. I'm in for it. What'd I do now?

"Why'd you tell Nurse Martha it's okay to come back next week? Costs thirty-seven dollars for her to come here, eat, drink tea, see if you can wiggle your toes and take one little peek at your arm."

"The cast comes off my ankle in a couple of days -- ." I attempt to ignore her question. Henrietta frowns at me. I sigh. "I think she needs the money and maybe she's a little lonely. That's all. It's probably a mistake."

"And next time you want to hide your friendship with Susan Ladona, you should say, 'Course I know her. She comes down every other week for tea and conversation.' Say you give her ideas for stories, or that she steals your ideas. Say that you're like sisters. No body'd believe a word of it."

I laugh, knowing she's right. "There was a time we told people we were sisters, even though we don't look a thing alike." My mind wants to drift, but I can't allow that. Tell her something safe.

"I've seen Susan just twice in the last twenty years. At the funeral after her brother was killed in Vietnam, and when her first novel was published. We write long letters every three or four months. Do you think nurse Martha will be saying anything?"

"Oh, probably that you're gay and Susan Ladona is a lesbian."

I watch her eyes dance, the hands on her hips, the defiant chin.

"Careful, Henrietta. Think about how she might refer to you in that case."

"She don't pay me no never mind a-tall." Then in the clipped southern accent of blue blood Virginia she adds, "Since when does being from Virginia make me a Yankee?"

"It's north of Georgia."

That's it. She tells me its my turn to fix dinner. I threaten to call out for pizza. In what I hope is mock exasperation, she relents and heads back to the kitchen. She returns carrying a tall lemonade for me and an iced tea for herself, places the glasses, sits in the other chair by the radio. She's waiting for an explanation of my behavior this afternoon. She'll know, the way a mother knows, if there's anything left out or if the truth's shaded.

"I'll tell you after supper."

Henrietta nods, turns on the radio, adjusts the volume. The "Queen of the Southern Psyche" introduction is made and the interviewer begins. Susan doesn't like the label, but doesn't mention it. Her voice, familiar, yet different, speaks from the box of plastic, wires and silicon wafers. The south Georgia drawl's gone, soft consonants its only trace. I don't hear either the vulnerability or the anger I'd remembered, but it's Susan.

"To Twain and Faulkner? Pretty good company. Add Stephen Crane and Flannery O'Connor and we'll have a real tea party."

"Everyone says that. Five feet one half inch. My driver's license says five one."

I cock my head and look at Henrietta who reads my meaning: Susan's stretching it.

"He's a musician, a cellist, with the New York Symphony Orchestra."

"Almost nineteen years. We've been too busy to get married, busy with life. I suppose we could tear down to city hall over the lunch hour and make things official for the government. There would be certain tax advantages, but we're happy the way we are."

"Living in New York City is like being a blood cell in a bear."

"Each of us works to keep our home healthy, happy, civilized. We have our specialized jobs, but we're part of much more. We travel through the arteries and pumping stations delivering energy and, in exchange, receiving our life. I've learned to enjoy people, even crowds of people."

"I'm always surprised that people ask me that question. It's perfectly consistent for ordinary people to commit extraordinary acts. We're capable of great heroism and the most demonic cruelty. I believe human beings have a tremendous capacity for both good and evil. And, yes, certainly these capacities can be combined in the same individual."

"No, I think a character without good and evil capacities would be merely a prop, like a piece of furniture in the story, certainly not a main character."

"Well, reseach for <u>Clog Dancer</u> took me to north Georgia, Tennessee, Kentucky, places you would expect, but also to pockets of cloggers as far away as the foothills of California's Sierras. The old gold rush town of Grass Valley.

"I tend to leave vengeance to fate, to God, if you prefer. We humans frequently compound mistakes when we try to set things right."

"Thank you. Yes, justice can be served by an unconcerned child, a negligent nurse, a snake or an alligator simply following nature's dictates. One's own body can be part of a death trap. Evil things happen to good people, too. There's no justice in that -- those times when God hides."

"That's right. The movie is due to be released in early spring."

"Well, the graphic descriptions in that novel came from medical people whom I promised anonymity. I simply put the descriptions in everyday words."

"Green? Yes and no. It means nothing special and many special things. When I wear green, my blue eye seems green. Actors like the 'green room' at the theater. It's the color of spring and trees, of jealousy and of money. Alligators and most snakes stand out better against a green background than a mottled brown one, live vegetation versus dead and dying. Some cottonmouths have a greenish cast to them."

"My eyes? People either stare or they look elsewhere after their first glance. Their reactions tell me more than they realize."

"You? You were great. You weren't uncomfortable with me at all."

"Your cousin, too? Ahh."

"Well, of course kids can be tough on each other, even when it's part of normal curiosity. I'd be asked what color my eyes were and whether or not I saw things differently out of each one. Things like that. In third grade, a new kid blurted out in class that I had witches' eyes. The teacher made him apologize, but it hurt.

"That next fall, when school began and we had to tell something about ourselves, about the summer, and all, I was ready. I'd planned my answer carefully, written it down and practiced it."

"I told them that each of my parents had given me the treasure of sight. My father gave me a dark brown eye, and my mother gave me a bright blue one."

"No, with snakes like the cottonmouth, the changing patterns of light are more important than color. In the water or on land, you rarely find a plain green background in the swamp, except maybe for a lily pad. The snake is colored to blend perfectly with the changing light and shadows."

"Yes. Cottonmouth's another name for the water moccasin. The inside of the snake's mouth is whitish. Most people never see the inside of that snake's mouth. If you do, it could be your last look."

My knuckles come up to my mouth. Henrietta looks at me. I glance back, trying to signify nothing in particular.

"Well, the reason more people are bitten by copperheads than water moccasins is that the water moccasins live in somewhat less accessible areas. Fewer people go into the swamps. Copperheads and hikers like the same terrain. Put your hand up on a rocky ledge in north Georgia somewhere, and you're likely to put it on a copperhead sunning itself. Also, the water moccasin is very shy. The moment a moccasin senses a human, it tries to flee. It's outta there -- unless it's cornered; then it'll try to kill you. All the same, when I was growing up, I didn't like being the first one to jump into the pond. I'd try to get my brother or little sister or the dog to be the first."

"No, not really. We'd usually toss in a rock. If we saw a snake swimming, we'd get our sticks and race around to capture it, when it came ashore."

"Thank you. It's been a pleasure."

"Too bad the interviewer didn't follow up more on some of her stories," Henrietta says. "Like those times God hides. You want me to leave this on while I set the table?"

"You can turn it off. Thanks. I want to think awhile."

3.

"You sure are taking a long time to finish that Ladona book that came in the mail," Henrietta says to me when I join her for the afternoon break we take on the back porch. She's sorting her recipe cards.

"Want to put those in a computer file?" I ask. Henrietta has had some computer courses, I've learned. "You can use my laptop and printer whenever you like."

"Believe I will. Thank you. So, what about the new Ladona book?"

I stare into the yard, shaded by three old pecan trees.

"Nuts are starting to fall. More than we can possibly use. And they're such a mess to shell. You know any children who'd like to gather some?"

"Uh huh. 'Course I do. I notice how you keep changing the subject when I ask questions. Don't you think it's time you told me about Susan Ladona?"

"Tonight after supper."

35

"Heard that before."

"Hot out here. Believe I'll go back inside."

"Uh huh."

I let the screen door slam.

The new cast with the rubber knob on the bottom works pretty well. Don't need the walker any more. I hobble to my room and close the door. Limp sheers are lifted away from the windows, but not a breath of air circulates. I swing up the heavy cast and flop on the bed. My hand gropes for a tissue to mop perspiration from my face. There's Susan's book on the night stand, unread. Breathe in, out, in again. Okay, admit it. Once I decide to tell Susan's story, I want to tell Henrietta my version. Susan's will vary in detail, interpretation and in the form imposed to make it a novel. I've lived with my version so long. . .

After supper, not wanting to draw any more bugs, we turn out the lights and sit in the big white wicker chairs on the screened-in porch, listening to the evening sounds. I weigh how much to share at a time. I want to stretch it out. Where to start? At last, I simply plunge in.

"I'd like to tell you her story straight out, Henrietta, but there're parts I'll have to fill in. Besides my role, there's Lucrecia, Susan's family and the dean. And the snake, the snake and the professor. Whenever I think of Susan, a snake's in the background, resting at the edge of memory, eyes intense, tongue waving, ordering its world.

"You said Susan's stories were filled with swamp creatures and it's true. Even in that radio interview they came up. She told me how the cottonmouth water moccasin and the copperhead strike without warning. The copperhead bites more people, but the cottonmouth kills more. Maybe that's why Southerners enjoy watching these two species in captivity. It's taken a while, but some of us have learned to leave them free."

I pause and think about what I've said. Henrietta brings me back. "Uh huh."

"Susan caught her first viper when she was seven, a ten inch baby cottonmouth, by the branch that runs close to one of the equipment sheds on her family's south Georgia farm. Caught it live. Nearly scared her poor mother to death. She kept it a week. Presented it to her uncle for his exhibits at his gator farm across the border, in Florida. It was small, but her uncle gave it a space.

"A couple more years and she was ready for serious snake hunting. You see, to understand Susan, to begin her story, we must go into the swamp."

Henrietta folds her arms and pulls her feet under her chair as I begin.

Both paddlers propel the canoe with silent figure eights, not breaking the surface. Susan and her uncle slide over the water, invisible in the night, following the familiar route from the farm, outside Waycross, skirting the wildlife refuge. They wear rolled kerchiefs around their heads to keep the rivulets of sweat from running into their eyes. In the dark, ten-year old Susan can distinguish the black cypress from the lighter blackness of the sky. The day's heat lingers through the night, an airless night, humidity nudging one hundred percent.

Susan's great-grandmother, a member of the Creek nation, bequeathed Susan her brown eye and the midnight hair that crowned the child and her uncle. Other ancestors were responsible for her blue-green eye, pale skin, and the freckles sprinkled across her nose and cheeks. Her spots of color, like those of their quarry, camouflage in the swamp, her uncle tells her. She likes that. She thinks of the swamp as a good place to hide and feels safe in its embrace.

The air hangs heavy with moisture, unmoving, but alive, loud with night music. The joyous, urgent sounds of the tiny creatures fill it with life. The insects sing as one, silent at a sound of paddle striking a stump or a call from a predator, then robust in full symphony, all listening, then singing, in unison.

The air is immobile, but not the land. At the edge of the Okefenokee, place of trembling earth, dense mats of vegetation form floating islands. Stalking birds ration their movements, unwilling to announce their presence too soon. People, walking in heavy boots, leave indentations that quickly fill with water, often unseen because the mats of fallen vegetation spring back as if no one had stepped there.

In cool weather, where there is open water, mist can be coaxed from the surface, but not this night. Susan sniffs the wet, musty smell of tannin, leached from the vegetation. She senses, without seeing, floating plants, bobbing with the ripples of their boat, and the grey Spanish moss, clinging from the bark and branches of the tall cypress trees above her head. In this place, water comes in all shades of black and brown, blackest ink at night, brown shades of murky tea in sunlight.

Probably no gators this close to civilization, all trapped and hunted out, first by the legal hunters, before 1937, then by the poachers, but sometimes nature can recover. In recent years, on the edges of the swamp, there'll be a gator roar, louder than a lion. Protected now, their numbers would come back. That's what the old swampers believed, and it seemed to be holding true. Every year the roars came closer.

Her uncle had anticipated the alligators' decline and worked to preserve them, combining some educational and conservation messages with his alligator ponds, the two-headed coral snake, key chains and coffee mugs at the sideshow on Highway 95, north of Jacksonville. Never mind what folks said of his younger days, her uncle had his legal licenses. He didn't do the gator wrestling any more, either. He had a couple of real strong fellows for that. Brave too, they understood it was important not to panic or show fear. Her uncle told her he hoped for a time when he could get the tourists to stop and see the exhibits and the gator ponds without having to entice them with man-gator wrestling and gator-gator wrestling over a cow leg bone or some such, at feeding time.

Course, Susan knew feeding time for gators is almost any time. In the hot weather, her uncle contracts with a poultry processing plant and a catfish farm on the coast, in addition to being willing to go and get any dead horse, cow, mule or whatever within fifty miles. His hauling fee's pretty cheap.

Henrietta wrinkles her nose at me, but she doesn't interrupt.

With long-handled snake hooks and sacks stowed at their feet, the paddlers are after vipers. Her uncle will sell all but the largest one or two specimens to other exhibitors. Susan and her uncle head for his staging area, where they will rest and make ready for the sun's light, not to bring the snakes out of the shadows -- that's not possible, but so the humans can see better.

True, they could capture moccasins closer to home. They don't have to go deep into the swamp, but the shelter and mystical beauty of Okefenokee calls them, holds them.

People frighten Susan more than snakes. Her parents worry about these swamping trips, but her uncle didn't, not any more. She has proved better than the others. She doesn't talk much and she doesn't mind going deep into the swamp in the dark. At dawn, they are in position.

Henrietta's arms are still folded tightly. She's watching the floor.

"Ever wonder how the snake must feel when it's captured?" I ask. She glares at me, but I go on.

"The forked tongue moves in and out, sensing, smelling a warm-blooded animal, a mouse. Close. The snake's tongue brings the scent back stronger with each flicking excursion. The snake sees the mouse's body heat, seeing, but not like people see things. The triangular head moves forward, investigating, over a smooth, hard obstacle. The body follows, but the supporting ground falls away! The snake struggles to cling to what seems like a thin tree limb. Thud! It lands in a dark sack with no way out. Trapped."

Henrietta flinches. "Just get on with it. Stop being silly. Trying to scare me."

By mid-morning, they have a snake in each of their sacks and start home, breaking their silence.

"Tell me, Suzy, what would you do if you had a mess of gators and snakes like I do?" Unk asks.

Susan rests her paddle and puts her chin in her hand, not answering for a while. "I believe I'd let them go, a few at a time, all over the swamp."

"And why would you do that?"

"So there would be enough food for them."

"No, I mean, why would you let them go, any of them? You've never let anything go that I know about."

"Well, one day I will. I wouldn't want to spend all my life in a pen or a glass case. Besides, I can catch more snakes any time I want to."

"That's the truth." Her uncle rubbed his stubbled cheeks. "Tell me, how's that pretty, blond mother of yours?"

Susan slumps. She bites the nail on her index finger before answering. "Kinda sad this past week."

"Again? Sorry to hear that."

"Yeah, she cries mostly. It makes me sad. Wish I knew what to do."

"Honey, it's not your fault. It's no one's fault. She gets those spells, that's all."

"It worries Daddy. He tries real hard to help her. When we do something she likes, she's happy for a moment, but she has this odd, happy, sad face. When I brought her that golden lily, from our last trip, and she was real pleased, I thought she was going to be okay, but then she sat down and gave me her shaky smile. I told her not to be sad. Everyone loves her. She told me she wanted to be happy, but she cried and then we cried together."

"I don't think she can help herself, Suzy, Hon. There's a streak of sadness in her family. I don't think she's strong enough to overcome it."

"I feel so lonely sometimes. Will -- will I be like mama?"

"You? No, Hon. You're strong, like the lily, beautiful and strong at the same time. This thing with your dear mama is the first of the tests you'll face, but you'll know the way. You understand the natural world. You'll escape the great sadness of your mother."

He begins chanting a Creek prayer. The swamp hushes to listen. Susan turns to watch him for a moment, and he catches the slight upturned expression of hope on her lips, despite her searching eyes.

Susan watches her mother pour white pills into a small canning jar with a two-piece lid. Her mother doesn't notice her until she speaks. "What're you doing, Mommy?"

"Saving these pills so I can get more, Darling. When the doctor gives me more, I put them in here instead of taking them."

"Why?"

"It makes me feel strong. With these, I'm in charge of my life. If a day comes when I'll need them, they'll be here, all in this jar. You mustn't tell anyone, not a soul. You hear?"

"Yes, m'am. But what are they for?"

"I just told you, Darling. They help me feel strong. I need to feel strong. It takes a long, long time to save them."

"Are you happy when you feel strong?"

"I guess I am. It makes me happy to feel strong."

"I like it when you're happy, Mommy."

"I do too, Honeybun, but if you tell anyone, I'll be so, so sad. You must never tell, not Daddy, or Sis, or your little brother, or Unk, or friends, or anyone. Promise?"

4.

"Explosive growth and decay constrict life cycles in the swamp. Life and death embracing, indistinguishable from each other."

I liked my beginning. Thought it was a good lead into this evening's story. Henrietta didn't.

"You going to get to the part where you met Susan?"

"Tomorrow evening."

"No. Tonight. Where did you meet? I got the swamp background."

Henrietta's schedule, not mine, I'm reminded. One more try.

"You know what Susan told me? Drowning tends to kill the fight. Gators prefer to drown their larger prey. They clamp down on a foot or something with their jaws and pull it under. Wait for it to die, then dine at their leisure."

"You can't let a night go by without mentioning the swamp, can you? I wonder who's more obsessed with alligators, you or Susan Ladona."

I ignore her and begin again.

"It was 1958. I was auditing a creative writing class that summer, one of the new teachers going back to school for additional units. My husband traveled all the time when we were first married. Scarcely knew I was away." I've said this too casually. Henrietta's look catches me for a moment, but I push on.

"The writing class was extra, for fun. The weather was hot, muggy, like today. I walked into the class with some of the students to find our prof sitting on his desk involved in an animated discussion with two other professors. They'd talk, bang the desk with a fist, laugh and direct each other to do this or that. It sounded like they were involved in an interdepartmental feud. On the board was a diagram, a plot continuum labeled front story, back story, with tangents, dead ends. It looked like someone was diagramming a sentence, except the tangents and dead ends were crossed out. Most of us copied the diagram into our notebooks while the professorial discussion ran well into class time.

"After a while, from their antics and gestures and the lowered tone, their conversation obviously changed. Jestin and the younger man watched the pretty girls, going so far as to raise an eyebrow and exchange a couple of furtive glances. I caught a

few sentences and imagined the rest to have been something like
--

'Stop leering at the freshmen. Your tongue's practically hanging out.'

'I'm not leering.'

'Got a pretty wife, you still interested in something on the side?'

'Cut it out. I just glanced at a couple of students coming through the door and this guy, of all people, lectures me.'

"'Pipe down, you two.' The elderly department chairman adjusted his glasses and turned to inspect us. On his way out, he resumed his former loud volume and said. 'Looks like the usual summer school group to me. Got to get back to the office. Ham, please let me know your Shakespeare class enrollment numbers by noon tomorrow.'

"Once the department chairman strolled out of earshot, Dr. Hamilton Jestin leaned his head closer to the man with the wedding ring and continued talking. Probably some advice like 'Act disinterested, bored. Let them think it's safe to approach you. Freshmen have so much to learn. Feed their fears. Overwhelm them with your superior knowledge and your helpfulness.'

"The other professor had turned his eyes back to the students. Dr. Jestin clapped his hand on the other man's shoulder, swung him partly around and pointing his finger in the other man's face, closed to his ear to say something like, 'And, never, never cut in on another professor's students,' as he directed him to the door, with a laugh and a shove.

"Dr. Jestin turned, glanced at the board and began erasing it. Apparently the diagram was from another class. Without apology or preamble, he began his lecture on the mechanics of writing and his methods for the class.

"The second day of class he had a semi-circle of students around his desk with whom he engaged in elaborate conversation, again beginning class late. The third class began with his putting a long schema for deconstructing writing up on the board. Late again, but only by six or seven minutes this time. By the fourth class, having set his pattern, he surprised us and began on time.

"Students wandering in three or four minutes late perturbed him into asking, 'What do I have to do about you students who come late?'

"'Start on time.' The answer that shot back startled him and he searched out the owner of the voice. None of the other students betrayed me by looking in my direction, but he guessed correctly and asked if I'd said it.

"I meant no disrespect, sir. I'm a teacher myself and know that if you begin on the minute, students will make a point of being here, ready."

"Ah, thank you, Miss -- ?"

"Mrs. Titch."

"'Mrs. Titch.' He glanced down at the enrollment sheet, with a smirk and a slight jerk of his head. I suspect the fact that I was auditing the course and not a lower classman he could bully was compensated by Titch's rhyming with bitch.

"Just out of high school, Susan Ladona and Lucrecia Barry, sat behind me. They were starting their freshmen course work early, and someone let them register for the creative writing class. They could have been sisters, both petite with silky black hair. That summer, Susan wore bangs and a long ponytail. Lucrecia's black hair waved over her left eye and fell into a soft pageboy at her shoulders. Each of them had the same dusting of freckles. Dark-eyed Lucrecia also came from south Georgia and knew Susan, although they had gone to different high schools.

"The three of us chatted during the break. As an older student, I might have made them feel less intimidated by the institution. They were surprised that I had spoken so bluntly to the professor. Susan told us how she hated to be called on in class.

"We talked about university life. Lucrecia was interested in learning to play bridge, a social prerequisite for everyone in college, she believed.

"Dr. Jestin came into the hall and glared at us, so I decided to drop the discussion. But, before I went to the drinking fountain, I told Susan and Lucrecia I'd come over to their dorm that night and we'd play some bridge.

"Perhaps it was our conversation, or maybe it was because she was a freshman, an attractive young woman with exotic eyes that could sparkle one moment and weep the next, but Dr. Jestin began to hound Susan, and other young women, in the sessions that followed. On our writing assignments, Susan's sentences were too long, then too short. 'Show, don't tell, Miss Ladona.'

'Cardboard characters.'

'Too many commas.'

'Give the reader a direct experience.'

'No flashbacks.'

'Write it all in one sitting to get it on the page. This reads like you've worked on it for ten years. It's over-written.'

'Use abbreviations.' Then 'Too many abbreviations.'

"Dr. Jestin made his points at Susan's expense, or Lucrecia's, or one of the other female students in the class. I can't remember his ever praising any of the young women, although several, like Susan and Lucrecia, were very earnest about their writing.

"He maintained a stale southern attitude toward women. He buried it deep. Sealed in a box, then a sheet of veneer. Waxed and polished with charm."

Henrietta said, "Uh huh. I know the type."

"His bias had a way of surfacing without telling him. In reaction to a raised eyebrow or frown. Easy enough to miss, to ignore. Not so the direct challenge, when a young woman questioned his interpretation or pulled the discussion off the narrow gauge he'd chosen. He didn't cultivate the prejudice. It was just there, a part of him like his eye color or a mole on his back. He embarassed himself sometimes. Making remarks that shut down discussion, making it dangerous.

"'You're always negative. If you can't learn from this, then I don't think very much of you.'"

"The only sign of inner tension, if it was that, the sudden unguarded flare at others that translated to, Hear me. Praise me. Bow over your notebooks.

"Me, he ignored completely. That was okay, I suppose. I admit I did learn in his class, before the problems surfaced. It's just that I might have learned more. I talked to a friend on the English faculty who told me Dr. Jestin's classes were always full. Maybe it was his obsession with mechanics. Students like to have formulas, and he gave us many.

"His favorite was for deconstructing writing. 'You get a certain thrust, fluency and power,' he would repeat, jabbing his fist at the class in an upper cut. Some of the guys snickered at his antics, finding them suggestive.

"For the first several evenings, Susan, Lucrecia and I met at the freshman dorm, reading our writing to each other then playing bridge with Lucrecia's roommate joining us until I had to leave at eleven fifteen, when the doors were locked. I knew I wasn't going to be able to keep up that kind of a schedule, and told them so, but college life excited them, and they would stay up talking after I left. How I wish I could have stayed to talk too. If there was a sign, a warning, we missed it.

"Dr. Jestin encouraged Susan, and others, to meet with him, one on one, to review their work. Students signed up for specific times. Susan's first appointment had to be changed, he told her. Perhaps late afternoon or early evening after supper. It was the only time his schedule wasn't filled.

"Susan went to the professor's basement office at five-thirty, her newly assigned time. The building reminded her of a tomb. The staff had gone home. He shredded her work, and she cried. She'd tried so hard. It seemed that her writing was worse, not better. He patted her hand, her arm, put his arm around her shoulders, encouraged more private sessions and was confident she would do better eventually.

"Susan told me how afraid she'd been. She didn't know what to do. Dr. Jestin dried her tears. He made her feel uncomfortable. She was not interested in him romantically. He was not unattractive, but close to three times her age and experienced at this game in ways she didn't imagine. I encouraged Susan to tell him the time wasn't good for her, to try for a time during the day when more people would be around.

"Apparently, Dr. Jestin seemed to prefer working with lower classmen. He didn't get them very often, except the occasional class and sometimes the summer creative writing course. He was a Shakespeare expert who usually taught upper classmen and graduate students. But I learned all this later.

"In class, I didn't interact with the other students much, feeling I'd bring Dr. Jestin's wrath upon anyone he saw with me. It was away from class that Susan, Lucrecia and I exchanged some of our work and tried to help each other. Susan had written some short pieces, about the Okefenokee. Her nature descriptions were among the best I'd read. One story she wrote told of running her canoe ashore and placing a foot onto ground that quivered and spoke to her. She wrote fanciful, delightful tales, innocent stories. Her work made me realize the swamp itself is a living creature, a marvelous creature that only wants to survive."

Henrietta gives me a look that warns I'd better not go off on a swamp tangent again. I ignore her.

"In Susan's earliest work, dragonflies, snakes, alligators were main characters. All of that changed. Dr. Jestin seemed kind of hard on her. He told her that personifying animals and insects was too improbable. No one would believe her. He'd guided many others. He could guide her. She needed to trust him."

Henrietta sucks her teeth and shakes her head. "Lordy, I bet I know where this story's going."

The long grass hasn't been cut in three weeks, and the bugs inhabit every inch of it. In the twilight, the first fireflies appear. We watch them for a while. They seem to hang in the moist air, signaling for an answer and the prospect of a mate. I love the fireflies, hate the chiggers, tiny, red creatures designed in Hell. My nails explore two-week old bites festering on my good ankle. Henrietta rubs her eyes.

"It wasn't just her youth and small stature that made Susan vulnerable," I say. "But that's for tomorrow night."

5.

"Susan felt terrible guilt about Lucrecia. Once she told me, 'My mother and I had a secret, just the two of us. I promised her I'd never tell, but she died, and after a while I told Lucrecia. It was that summer when we first went up to college. The secret killed her. I killed my friend.'"

"What was the secret?" Henrietta asks. She is tracing the scar between her jaw and ear.

"On one of our bridge nights, Susan and Lucrecia continued to talk after Lucrecia's roommate and I left. Susan told me about their conversation, later, when it was too late."

"'I've never told a living soul, so you have to swear you won't either. Swear?'" Susan asked.

"'I swear,'" Lucrecia said.

"'I brought something to campus with me. Something that was my mother's. Don't know why. Maybe because she believed they gave her power over her life. They didn't though. She died anyway.

"'I've heard the whispered gossip. People say her crash was a suicide, but Daddy doesn't want anyone to talk about it. He won't let us talk about how she died. I think he feels suicide is something to be ashamed of. I don't feel that way. Wish Daddy and I could talk about it. You think suicide's a sin?'"

"'No, I don't believe that,'" Lucrecia said. "'We can't judge someone else's troubles. We don't know what other people might be facing. My cousin's best friend committed suicide. I don't believe he's in Hell for it. He was in hell then, living.'"

"'It's a jar, a small jar.'"

"'What is?'"

"'What I brought with me from home. I saw my mother with it just once, but she seemed happy, so I brought the jar with me. I knew right where she kept it. Where she hid it. I was the only other person who knew, until now. Promise you'll keep it secret.'"

"'I promise.'"

"'I think I took it so I could have something that made her happy. But it didn't work in the long run. Didn't work for her. It won't work for me. Don't know why I took it.'"

"'Jeez, Susan. What is it? What's in the jar? You're worrying me. Where is it?'"

"'It's in my room upstairs. I'll show you. It's not dynamite or anything.'"

"They crept along the dim hallway to the single room at the far corner of the dorm's second level, careful not to wake the others on the floor. Lucrecia wiped her sweaty palms on her skirt. No one else seemed to be awake or about. Susan went to her closet and took down a shoe box from the shelf. Inside, wrapped in tissue paper was a small canning jar and the pills."

'Probably sleeping pills,' Lucrecia said.

'Yeah, probably.'

'Lots of 'em.'

'Forty-seven.'

'You should get rid of them.'

'I know, but I can't. Not yet.'

"We gave up our evening bridge sessions. Summer school began hitting like a thunderstorm, pelting us with heavy homework assignments. Later, Susan told me that at first, she felt grateful to Dr. Jestin. Much of what he said about her work made sense to her. She was determined to apply each suggestion. For the second individual session, he opened his date book of inked-in squares. Too busy during the day. His place was a natural setting, peaceful, inspiring, he suggested. She hesitated, but he again mentioned how busy he was. It simply was the only convenient time. Susan became flustered, sensing something wrong, then convincing herself she was being silly. Dr. Jestin assured her he was solely interested in his students' work and helping them become good writers. He could help her if she were willing to make the effort. Grades were very important at the University, A's critical, for an aspiring writer, he said. They set the second meeting.

"For Susan it was a confused, brutal evening. He talked to her of direct experience, risk-taking, a sense of leaping off into a story, not knowing where it'd lead. There'd been champagne. It was 1958, and she was naive. She did resist, but all her past teachers had been trustworthy, encouraging. Susan also didn't know Dr. Jestin pursued several young women simultaneously. He seemed to enjoy the challenge, almost like he was going after some kind of record.

"She had wanted to write about a mother-daughter relationship, she told him. Her mother had died in a car crash when Susan was in eighth grade, and she still grieved. Everyone believed it was suicide. Her mother had gone off the road at a turn, right into a tree, at high speed, no skid marks. She wasn't under the influence of anything, except her internal sadness.

"Dr. Jestin urged Susan to try something completely different, a love scene. You can imagine how it went."

Henrietta waves her hand and sucks her teeth in disgust. She refolds her arms. "Poor, stupid child. Never should have gone to his place."

"He took her hand, asked her to describe her feelings. She hedged. He kissed her fingertips, asked her to try harder. Did she feel a tingling sensation? Try harder. Where? 'Think of this as an experiment. Record what your body is telling you. Uneasy? No, try to feel tenderness. The ability to record sensations honestly is fundamental to good writing. The difference between a great writer, or a merely average one. You're young, don't know how to relax. I can teach you to feel, to trust your senses.'

"She squirmed and told him she was nervous, uncomfortable. He poured another small glass of champagne, telling her champagne wasn't really wine. Coming from a teetotalling family from south Georgia, she suspected otherwise, but didn't want to be impolite."

Henrietta raises both her hands to the heavens and slaps them together.

"Susan moved to his stereo, thumbing through his records, putting distance between herself and Dr. Jestin. He urged more champagne, told her to select music for romance. 'Set the scene,' he coaxed, giving her a long lead. 'What about lighting? Play the main character. See the room through her eyes. What about this room could be used romantically? Which colors? Why? How does the view of the lake enhance the mood? The woods? Scary? A hiding place? I'll protect you.'

"Too late she felt the trap. The hair on her arms and the back of her neck stood up. He came too close. Fear panicked her. She was four feet eleven and a half inches. The professor enveloped her in a bear hug, crushing her lips with his heavy mouth. She squirmed, her ears rang with her own voice screaming, 'No. I don't want this. No.' She began to gag on his after-shave lotion, the vestiges of stale cigarette smoke in his shirt, dust.

"She saw the cream-colored ceiling, the overstuffed furniture, the room whirling. Her head banged on the floor.

'Think of your story,' he said. 'Relax and think of your story.'

"She continued to struggle, another 'No!' He paused, drew back, raised his fist and punched her in the solar plexus. She couldn't breathe, thought that he'd kill her. He knew exactly what he was doing. She squeezed her eyes shut, trying to escape, but her detached mind watched anxiously, as if from the ceiling or one of the chairs across the room.

"'Shouldn't have made me hit you, but you'll be okay. Don't do anything foolish when you get back to campus,' he said. He talked in a normal, congenial tone, so matter of fact. He joked that it would appear that she'd come alone to his home, uninvited. Reviewing her work wasn't much of a story. He was a respected professor. She was a silly freshman, experimenting.

Her appointment was inked in his book for three in the afternoon, he informed her. She'd missed it.

"He told her to imagine what people in her home town would think? At her church? He reminded her how people love to talk in small towns. Attacked? Surely it was her own fault, if it really happened that way. Who'd believe her? Her poor father would be so ashamed. Through her tears, she knew he was right. Or, thought she knew.

"He said she was going to miss lockout if she didn't leave soon. "I could call, say I'm your father and sign you out for the night. Give you a chance to compose yourself." The way he looked at Susan made her stomach lurch. She snatched her purse and darted for the door.

"The next morning, I dropped into a coffee shop for a quick breakfast. Susan was in the back booth. I startled her. She wanted to avoid people. Dark glasses couldn't cover the signs of crying. A purple bruise marred her right temple, more bruises around her mouth. Purple lines above and below her lips, and a small scratch on her left cheek. A handprint around her right wrist, more bruises on her left wrist. When I asked what happened, she disintegrated. We cut our classes. She couldn't explain all the marks, even later that afternoon, after she'd told me everything.

"Worst of all, Jestin expected her to return. He'd talked more about her writing. When she told me, she kept repeating, 'As if he were doing me some kind of favor.'

"I remember her hands shaking, hot coffee spilling, burning her fingers, tears dropping on her blouse, the frightened, tiny voice, far away. I urged her to call her father, but she wouldn't, and she refused to let me call him. Too embarrassed and fearful.

I suggested we go to the University authorities. Bad advice. We should have gone to the police. In those days, that town, they might not have been any better, but we'll never know.

"She didn't want to go to the University President's office or the campus police, either. She didn't want to talk to anyone else, but she didn't stop me when I went to call the Dean of Women's office. Yes, they'd see us right away. I practically carried her to the dean's office. The secretary regarded us suspiciously, like lepers, a forerunner of the reception we received from the ex-Army WAC, who didn't let me stay with Susan while she was interviewed. The ordeal further traumatized her. When the dean suggested she be checked into the infirmary, I thought it was to help her. Their idea of help was sedation.

"The dean said Susan was to have no visitors, but later, I told the staff I was her sister and bluffed my way in. A nurse became suspicious when Lucrecia arrived later that afternoon and also claimed to be her sister. Lucrecia was more believable than I, but we managed it, though the nurse refused to leave us alone with Susan.

"Lucrecia said she went to the housemother for Susan's dorm key as soon as she learned that she was in the infirmary. She thought Susan would like to have her teddy bear, toothbrush, a few things. 'I've cut one class and I'm late for another,' she said. 'The house mother said Susan fainted or something. I'll call you tonight around nine, so you can tell me what really happened.' And she was gone.

There wasn't any good place to talk privately, to tell her. The quick conversation, posing as sisters at Susan's bedside, was our last. I still see Lucrecia's sweet face with the freckles across the small nose, the tiny, pink mouth and the big, dark eyes. I never saw her again. Neither of us did.

Linda Lanterman

6.

This afternoon Henrietta sits at the side table in the kitchen nook where I've set up the computer. She uses a spreadsheet program with more expertise, or at least more fluidly than I. "Next time I get stuck, I'm calling you," I say.

"Uh huh. Ought to know it. I've had a course or two on this." She wraps up her work and swivels her chair to face me. "What happened to Lucrecia?"

"That's for after supper."

"No. It's for now."

I pull out a chair opposite her and pinch the end of my nose to stop the tingling. My eyes mist up. "I can't tell you exactly. Just what I surmised. What I believe."

"Before I returned to Atlanta after summer school, I went out to the pond where nine gracious, old homes encircled the water and lawns shaded by mature trees flowed down to the edge. On a visit to a neighboring house, an acquaintance I knew, I saw it.

The whole layout. A quiet, beautiful place of evil. Where Dr. Jestin lived. One or two other faculty members, a couple of the town's leaders. It isn't hard to imagine what happened to Susan or what happened to Lucrecia."

The breeze wafted intermittently in the darkness. It bounced sounds across the water, unobstructed until filtered on the opposite shore by the piney woods and a few dogwoods, all leafed out. The delicate trees framed an ancient farmhouse, remodeled and expanded, in character. Built long before air conditioning, the house's orientation took advantage of the prevailing summer breezes, the view of the pond a minor consideration.

Short, stabbing cries and pleading sobs floated across the water, through a screened window, fluttering the white sheers tied back to bid the messenger enter. The sleeping woman's brain worked to make sense of the cries, more suggestions than sounds. She moved her head. The air current wafted again, so gently it did not disturb a strand of hair across her cheek, but the sound of terror reached her ear. Her eyes opened wide. Her body tensed, trying to hear it again. Nothing. She propped her head on one elbow to listen.

"Bad dream?" her husband asked.

"Listen a second."

"Probably a cat," he said.

"No, something else."

"No more scary movies." The man wrapped his arms around his wife to comfort her and fell asleep. The woman eased herself from his grasp and continued to listen until sleep overtook her. A wail of anguish, broken and dispersed, reached her, but sleep was too strong. Only her unconscious heard.

The woman brought her iced tea and her novel out to the chaise in the dog trot, the breezeway between the main wings of the house. Most of her work completed, she wanted to rest a few minutes with her feet up. In spite of the tea and her book, she dozed. The breeze came, light but steady.

A yell, then a high-pitched, nervous laugh awoke her. She glanced out to the floating dock and diving board in the middle of the pond. She heard words and could see two people in the water.

"I didn't touch you. Don't scream like that!"

"A fish bit me! Right on the back of my knee! They're nibbling at my legs."

The woman recognized Hamilton Jestin, the English professor from the house across the water, but she didn't recognize the girl. She took the birding glasses from the drawer in the side table and trained them on the two people splashing in deep water and hanging onto the dock. Yes, it was Dr. Jestin and a young woman with black, shoulder length hair. For a moment she remembered the cries in the night and frowned, but she shook her head and put the small binoculars away.

The air currents carried "No skinny dipping!" from the girl and the woman looked up again. She thought of her as a girl, someone far too young for the professor. The woman watched him pull something that might have been his swimming trunks from the dock and struggle with them in the water. The professor took off after his companion who was swimming for the shore in front of his home. The woman had heard the rumors about Dr. Jestin, and, living where she did, she gave them credence. Again she thought of the sounds in the night. Not the same. Not like today's.

When she was preparing supper and chatting with her newly tenured husband, a cry shot through the window and ricocheted off her kitchen walls. "Oh, dear God," the woman whispered and buried her mouth and nose in her hands. Tears ran from the corners of her eyes. She urged her husband to call the professor. He refused, telling her Dr. Jestin was a nice sort. Besides, he had seniority in the department, and his escapades with his co-eds weren't any of her business. The husband crumpled his newspaper under his arm and stalked to the den.

She telephoned anyway. Was anything wrong? She'd heard cries. Dr. Jestin spoke in reassurances. The wife hung up and vomited in the sink. The wind died.

Linda Lanterman

7.

"I didn't know Lucrecia made no phone call that evening. I'd gone back to the infirmary to visit Susan. My efforts didn't do much good. She was in a drugged sleep most of the time. The next day, when Susan was awake, a huge woman with curly, dyed red hair and tight nurses uniform, brought us the news along with Susan's lunch tray.

"Lucrecia Barry, our friend, the beautiful young woman who actually could have been Susan's sister, had been found dead, apparently a suicide, sleeping pills, probably.

"'Didn't know her, did you?' The nurse was bustling about the room.

"I sat down hard, missed the seat of the metal chair and toppled with it to the floor, where I stayed, leaning against the wall. I remember telling the nurse I was fine, didn't want to get up. The floor was polished, waxed linoleum, grey with multi-colored flecks, smooth to touch. There was a large, torn cobweb on the metal framing under Susan's bed. Rubbing alcohol and antiseptic assaulted my nose. The nurse helped me to the righted chair and dabbed at the long, red scratch on my leg.

"'Yes, we do. We know her. We have Dr. Jestin's creative writing class together," I said.

"'You knew her? Oh, dear. I didn't mean to -- Oh dear.'

"We learned that Lucrecia had missed classes for two days. Her roommate reported her missing the first night. The nurse's husband had seen the body. He had been downtown delivering chemicals to the coroner's office when they brought her in.

"Susan had started hyper-ventilating. 'What -- ? How --? Lucrecia? No, God, no! No! I should've warned her. -- thought I was the only. . .' The redheaded nurse called for assistance. The doctor ordered more sedatives for Susan, took my arm, shoved me toward the door, told me to leave.

"I drove over to the dorm and went up to Lucrecia's room on the third floor. Her roommate opened the door and stood there with red-rimmed eyes and a tissue pushed against her nose. We hugged each other, sobbing. She was packing.

"'My parents are driving over to pick me up this afternoon. They don't want me here a minute longer. I always wanted to attend this University. I never thought it would be this, this -- ' She looked around the room hopelessly. 'I have notes for you and Susan from Lucrecia. Will you get Susan's to her?'

"She handed me two sealed envelopes, one with my name, one with Susan's. Lucrecia's roommate said, "I had one too, but the police kept it when I showed it to them, so I didn't tell them about these.'

"That evening I went to the small cafeteria in the basement of the infirmary. No food service, only a couple of vending machines. Put in my coins and watched dark coffee splash into a paper cup coming unglued as it filled. Curly Red walked up behind me and said, 'Better meet me at Poss' Barbecue. Least they have real cups.'

"The parking lot at Poss' was jammed. I found Red inside seated in a booth, waiting for me. I slid across patched leatherette and leaned over the table to hear her above the jukebox.

"'Had your supper?' she asked. 'Good barbecue here. Fast service.'

"'Just coffee.'

The spicy barbeque smell, the smell of any food, made me sick at heart. Red ordered and while she ate, we talked.

"'I could get fired being friendly to you, let alone talking to you about this. Don't say anything, please.' I nodded and she continued. 'It makes me so mad. The University hides its dirty laundry and pretends nothing has ever happened. When they're caught, they're worse, always saying the girls are loose tramps who wanted to have sex. Or, the girls should have understood how they tempted the poor football player, or in this case, the poor professor.' Her teeth cracked the rib bone she was working on, splattering her nose and cheek with barbeque sauce. Two specks flew across the table to the front of my white blouse.

"She wiped thick, red sauce from her cheeks onto her napkin and continued eating while she detailed many of the rape cases she'd seen over the past several years. But they were anecdotal and hearsay, without the specific names which were sealed -- or destroyed -- by the University for privacy. I didn't know how to help Susan, where to turn.

I telephoned my husband, then my father-in-law. They both advised me to leave it alone. I'd done all that could be expected. They told me how I could lose my job, maybe even my teaching credential, for being meddlesome. I was not a witness. I'd be considered a troublemaker. Both of them mentioned the rumor mills that existed in the connections among the superintendents throughout the state. I'd never get another good recommendation. My husband reminded me of a case where we lived that was similar."

"You're biting your nails," Henrietta says to me. "Quit doing that."

I rush on, grasping, out of ideas. We've had our supper and finished the dishes. Leaving the hot kitchen, we head for the screened porch. There's no breeze, but the twilight seems cooler. I begin without Henrietta's prompting.

"In her last book there was a passage. I noticed a passage, that jumped off the pages at me. It had to be part of her own story, but she'd woven it into another. I'll read it to you, if you'll get the light."

"Uh huh," she says. I snatch the book from the little wicker side table and fumble for one of the places I'd marked.

"This is from <u>Death at Big Muddy</u>."

"I can see that," she says. I start reading aloud.

The old campfire the poachers used, caught the breath of a whisper though the dry grass, one of the whispers the dusk sends, announcing itself. The whisper whirled among the rocks, the breath growing hot, a tiny lick of flame. Angry, a demon roared to life and flew into the air. Another, more insidious, ignited the earth itself.

The fire had to burn itself out with the help of thunderstorms, but hundreds of acres were fouled. The swamp recovered, except the place where the demons emerged was never again the place it had

> *been. The land itself had burned, leaving new hollows for the waters to fill when the wet season came. Islands that had been landmarks disappeared.*
>
> *Dora, the dragonfly, saved her friend, Elita, the snake, by instructing her to stay in the water. Elita obeyed, coming to the surface only to breathe. But, the fire turned her back almost black and it was a long time before Elita found a new home, a place where she could live once again among friends and feel comfortable.*

I finish and look at Henrietta. She returns my look and waits. "Uh huh," she says at last.

"It's an analogy."

"I think you're changing the subject again. That's what I think. Uh huh."

"Well, Henrietta, of course nothing changes the fact that I wasn't much help to Susan. I didn't know how to help her. Didn't know what else to do. Don't you see?"

She doesn't meet my eyes. "I had a lot of growing up to do, a lot to learn about courage. Not that anything I might have done would have helped Susan in that era. Such a closed, cruel society."

Henrietta stares at the deepening darkness and runs her finger along the length of her scar. "Don't have to tell me about what kind of society it was in 1958, nor what it's like now. But it's some better than it was.

"I'm going in for a minute. Can I get you anything?" she asks, pushing herself up with two hands on the arms of the chair and switching off the porch lamp as she starts into the house.

"Some ice water, please -- and your story," I say.

She stops, straightens, and looks at me, her chin leading. "Cooking and caring. Helping folks."

"I mean everything."

She looks at me mouth open, her tongue probing a molar. "It's not a nice story."

"Neither's mine."

"All right, then." She goes into the house, and I listen to the crickets who have taken over the night. We'd negotiated, we both understood, her story for the rest of mine.

Her apron pocket bulges with tissues when she comes back with my ice water and another iced tea for herself. She settles, pulls a tissue from the wad in her pocket, and says again, "It's not a nice story, Miss Vivian."

A tear, caught in starlight, escapes down her cheek. Maybe I shouldn't have pressed.

Linda Lanterman

8.

"My second husband started drinking white lightning after we were married. Spent every cent he could get on it. He didn't want me to study. Began threatening me. It got worse when I enrolled in a correspondence course. Saved the fee out of my food money for seven months, totin' leftovers from the sorority house to keep us fed, which the house mother allowed, so long as it was nothing too big."

Henrietta pauses. "No, guess I need to start before that.

"When I was a child, I didn't honestly believe that there were good white people. What I have to say is, I'd never experienced one for myself. The preacher, my teachers, my parents, the old people would say things like race doesn't matter when it comes to good and bad, and that there were not enough good people and too many bad ones, no matter what their color. They always said things like that. I knew the words, but where I lived there were no white folks that I cared to know.

"Looking back, I suppose you could say I had, what we call today, an attitude. Like your Professor Jestin, only different. And that might be true, but if it is, then I'd have to add that maybe I was reflecting a whole lot of white attitudes that I'd seen. You might also say that I didn't know my place. Uh huh. But I did. White people saw a Negro girl, they didn't see me. I didn't like getting assigned a place when no one asked me or my people about it.

"I learned plenty about place when I started school. I liked school. Don't remember when it was that I realized that no white kids went to our school. It wasn't long.

By the time I was in high school, I understood the entire system. I understood about the old textbooks, the rundown buildings, the broken desks. I knew that one white man, the superintendent, and his staff, ran all the schools. When he retired, our teachers had to contribute to his gift, but no black folks, not even Old Mr. Johnson, our principal, were invited to his farewell reception. Social mixing wasn't allowed.

"I saw the new white high school being built, a pretty, brick, two story building with thirty-eight classrooms stretched out on each side of the main portico, seventy-six in all. Their school had a long, circular drive and large green lawns. People said there was a big library, full of books and brand new tables and chairs. The school had a modern chemistry laboratory, with little sinks and gas jets for every two students. I saw a picture of it in the newspaper.

"The gym connected to the main building by a long, curving, covered walkway, and the athletic fields stretched for acres and acres with separate fields for football, baseball and track. They had tennis courts and a swimming pool. The junior ROTC had a small building behind the main building, adjacent to the fields.

"I knew the truth of it when I heard the explanation for the high school's taking up so much land. The new school separated the old, historic white neighborhoods from the area some folks called Darkie town. They needed lots of land to do that, to create a physical barrier between the neighborhoods. A lifetime later, it seemed, when integration finally did come, it was instant. I got a good laugh about it too, but it was a bitter laugh.

"But, my time was earlier, way before Brown v. the Board of Education in 1954, which scared the white folks into buying new books for black children and fixing up some of our buildings. I attended segregated schools. I did my lessons and tried to learn everything. I worked hard, but one real important lesson I learned outside of class, from a white girl.

"I'd seen her once before, after school, a white girl about my age, waiting for the Broad Street bus. One day there she was again. She saw us coming, but before we got to her, I stopped my two girl friends and whispered a plan.

81

"'White folks always expect us to get off the sidewalk for them. She's by herself. Let's see what she does when we take up the whole sidewalk. Spread out.'

"I wasn't prepared for her reaction. She had this kindly expression on her face, a tentative smile. When she stepped off the granite curbing into the street, she looked me right in the eye. She understood the whole game. It made me mad! Two steps past her, I stopped, turned around, put my hands on my hips and demanded to know her name.

"'Lori Jean,' she said. 'What's yours?'

"Just like that, she answered me. Her voice was nice, not haughty, or brash. I couldn't believe her reaction and kept pushing, maybe not as hard. 'Mine's Henrietta. You go to that new high school?'

'Yes.'

'What year are you?'

'I'm a freshman. How about you?'

'I'm a senior. These are my friends. She's a senior, and this one's a junior.'

'Really? Seniors don't even talk to freshmen at my school. They're too stuck up.'

"I asked her why she was waiting there, and she said she was waiting for the bus to take her home. Her family had moved to town recently. I told her I was born there. She asked about my favorite courses. My friends watched a while and went on. While Lori Jean and I talked, I realized I wasn't angry any more. She was just a kid like me. It was the first time I understood I resented a person's whiteness, but not her. Knowing that and letting go of the resentment are two different things, though.

"I'd see Lori Jean every now and then, at the bus stop, and we'd chat, but after that year, I didn't see her any more. You might say it wasn't much of a friendship, but we'd both crossed the color line, and we were better people for it. I know I was. My first white friend moved away. It was a long time before I had another."

Henrietta paused. We listen to the night for a while, before she continues.

"My first husband, the father of my three children, died in an auto accident, like yours. I loved him. He was a good man. God sure was hiding when that car hit him." She wipes her eyes with the palm of her hand, blows her nose in a tissue and clears her throat.

"My second husband --. He -- he was bad. I didn't know it when I married him, but he was. I -- I came home from work one night in the rain and found my little son in the crib with the baby and heard my daughter calling me. Crying out for me. Crying for her stepdaddy to put her down. She was five, a baby of five. He had his hand in her panties, carrying her around the room, swinging her around. He was touching her. Not like a father should touch a child. Not like a stepfather should touch a child. No one should touch a child like that."

Henrietta wipes her nose, rubs her eyes, then rubs her finger tips along her hair line. She moans and the tears flood out. The crickets stop singing. Night closes around us. She takes out more tissues. I reach over to pat her shoulder. "Oh, Henrietta."

The tears stop. Her chin comes up. "He saw my face and put her right down. I hit him. Yelled and hit him along side the head with my big purse, hard as I could. He fell to the floor. I grabbed my baby girl and went into the other room. She was clinging to me, little arms tight around my neck, sobbing her eyes out. I wrapped her up in her little blanket.

"I heard my husband getting to his feet in the other room, cussing, drunk and cussing. I put my baby down in a chair and stood in front of her. I was going to kill him, if he tried to get her. I told him to get out, get out and never come back.

"He laughed. He staggered toward me. I'm a big woman. I wasn't afraid of him. He told me to get away. The baby cried harder. Screaming. He caught my hand and swung me around, holding me tight from behind. I'd forgotten his knife. Said he was going to cut my throat. Poked the point in just below my chin to prove he meant it.

"'You'll hang!' I knew hanging scared him. Two of his cousins were hanged, and it scared him good. 'They'll find you and hang you just like Frank and Jesse.'

"'Yeah, they might,' he said. 'This is to remind you not to bother me no more. Hear? You bother me any more, and your little girl'll get the same thing.'

"He cut me. Ran the point of his ugly knife from my chin to my ear. It wasn't the sting so much as the sound that terrifies. I could hear my skin tearing. But I wasn't dead. He turned me loose and laughed at me, holding my face together, trying to stop the hemorrhaging. He left the house and I ran to my neighbors, begged them to hide my daughter and little boys. One neighbor was a good nurse who told me my little girl would be all right, physically, but that I needed to get my face sewed up at the hospital. I didn't know if Mrs. Cloverlee would help me, but I used my neighbor's telephone and called the sorority house.

"Mother Cee?" I asked. Of course, it was. Henrietta doesn't bother to answer.

"She came for me in her car and took me to the emergency. She told the white doctor I cut myself when I slipped in the kitchen. He had some questions, but I told him it hurt to talk, which was true.

We stopped at the sorority house on the way back. Mrs. Cloverlee unlocked the pantry and told me to take what I needed.

If the house wouldn't grant it, she'd pay for it, she told me, and she went and got some paper sacks.

"On a bottom shelf, in the back, with the bleach, detergent and furniture polish, I saw some rat poison. Mrs. Cloverlee saw it too. 'Take anything you need, anything at all," she said. So I dropped the poison in one of the sacks.

"She wrapped up a piece of peach pie, left over from supper and gave me more fresh peaches and milk for the children. It was past midnight when Mrs. Cloverlee took me home and told me to take the day off, if I needed to. I was scheming, in the hospital, in the car.

"I stayed up. Made another peach pie, browned the upper crust a little darker than usual and left it in the pie safe, one piece gone. In the morning, I took the milk and two tins of tuna over to my nurse friend's and talked with her daughter who was watching my kids, then I went back and waited.

"The slice of pie from the sorority house was at my place at the table, a bite missing, a fork on the plate. I set the trap for him and he came walking right into it, just like I knew he would.

"'Take the kids to your mother's?' he asked.

"'Umm,' I said, not looking at him.

"'Got your face stitched up. That's good. It won't be too bad.'

"I ate a bite of pie.

"He glanced around for my purse. 'They give you the day off? You get paid yesterday?'

"'Umm.'

"'I need a couple of dollars. Any more pie?' He walked to the pie safe, took out the pie, took a fork from the drawer and began eating straight from the pie tin. 'Get me a couple of dollars now, you hear, Henrietta. I need a couple of dollars.'

"I looked at him for the first time. Glared at him while he licked his fingers. A fork in one hand and he still used his fingers. I went to get two dollars from my purse, but he'd followed me and grabbed all the cash I had. I left him to it and went back to my pie. He laughed, counted the bills and sat down. He demanded coffee and ate the rest of the pie, the whole thing.

"His mood changed. Became very pleased with himself. Said how nice it was having a wife to wait on him and not talk back the way I did before. He said he was going out again and didn't know when he'd be back.

"'I expect my whole family to be here and a good supper ready.'

"I watched him fold the bills in two and shove them in his pants pocket and go out the door.

"I was at the sorority house when the police came to tell me they'd found him in the river. Been dead about two days. They'd found a jug of white lightning too, mostly gone. They believed it

87

was his. He drowned, they said. Mrs. Cloverlee sat me down and shushed the police. They politely said they were sorry and departed. And, that was that. No one cared too much about some ol' drunk colored man who got himself drowned in the river.

"The house gave him a simple coffin and a burial. Bless her heart, Mrs. Cloverlee asked for more money in her food budget for me and my children. At Christmas, the children were invited for a special party and presents from the chapter. I'd really misjudged some of those girls. It touched my heart to see them with my children and to see my little girl so happy."

"I think your children were grown by the time I was there, Henrietta. I don't remember hearing about any of this."

"It was long ago," she says.

We concentrate on other details to avoid the issue of premeditated murder. "Your daughter, was she okay?"

"Yes. My friend and I explained to her that what happened to her -- it, it wasn't her fault. That it wasn't proper for her stepfather, or any one to touch her like that. We told her to tell us if anyone ever did again. We also told her that he was gone forever. I praise God that she wasn't harmed permanently. I beg understanding and forgiveness for what I did, but Lord help me, I'd do it again.

"The times being what they were, the coroner accepted the police report. Didn't bother with the body. That was to my advantage. They put him in a box and put the box in the ground. The marker's gone, I heard. Wasn't much of a marker in the first place. Can't say that I tended the grave, either.

After a few moments, she says, "Nuff of old troubles. Tomorrow you tell me the rest of Susan's story."

Linda Lanterman

9.

"The campus infirmary stay wasn't any help. There was no counseling, unless you call the visit from one of President's administrative assistants, counseling. He came the next morning when Susan was alone. Ignoring her bruises, the man insinuated that Susan was a troublemaker, making up some wild story for her creative writing assignment.

"Confused and furious that he blamed her for everything that happened, Susan cried and asked to know more about Lucrecia. He seemed to imply to her that at least her friend had the good grace to kill herself. When I arrived, the redheaded nurse was cradling Susan in her arms, stroking her hair as she would a little puppy.

'I found her chanting some kind of nonsense and rocking back and forth,' Red said. 'She's had a good cry.'

"Anger replaced the chanting and crying, which seemed to me to be healthy. Susan asked me to return for her in her car and gave me her keys. She was determined to check herself out of the infirmary. Since I was over twenty-one, we pushed further the lie that I was her sister, but the University didn't want to release her, except to a parent. But we had them on this. We said our father was an unpredictable, redneck, south Georgia farmer who carried his twelve gauge everywhere. He'd shoot up the whole school if he knew what happened to his favorite daughter.

"I only met the poor man once, years later. The description was unkind, but effective at the infirmary.

"That was the bottom for Susan, but she was through with crying. She'd begun to smolder with a cold, burning determination.

"The more people who knew, the more likely the University would find itself and one of its professors in the newspapers. They had weathered such incidents before and did not regard ours as much of a threat, but we persisted and Susan was released.

"Susan's car was a little Ford Falcon, a rehabilitated wreck, her father had bought at the auto auction. It had been repainted in a pale, robin's egg blue, the universal color for repaint jobs in those years. Whenever I saw her driving that car, I had the impression it wanted to go down the road sideways. I guess it was okay mechanically, and I suspected it was just cheap, summer transportation. Freshmen couldn't have cars during the regular term. I thought her father probably would either keep it for her, or resell it, if he could get a deal on something better.

"We drove to her dorm where I'd left my car, but we didn't go inside. Lucrecia was dead, and her roommate had gone home. I remembered the note Lucrecia's roommate had entrusted to me and pulled it from my purse. Susan ran her fingers over the familiar handwriting that spelled out her name, then opened the envelope."

I found out why you are in the infirmary. Have strength for both of us. Write to me when you think of me. Somehow I'll know.

I feel so dirty, so ashamed. God will make me clean again.

Lucrecia

"I watched her read the note, then stare out the windshield. 'So he attacked her too.' Susan folded the note and put it in her blouse pocket, over her heart. Tears flooded down my face. My nose ran. I had one, useless, crumpled tissue. I began mopping my face with my cotton shirt sleeve, but Susan had finished her crying.

"'Stop it! You aren't helping anyone by blubbering like that. Don't you have another class this afternoon? You'd better get going.'

"I protested to no avail. Calmly, she put on her sunglasses."

"'You are going. Yes, you are. We're going to appear as normal as possible considering a friend of ours just died. That'll excuse your red nose and eyes. Now get going.' Susan gave me a hard shove, pushing me into the car door.

"She was going to drive to the river, see if she could find the place where they'd found Lucrecia's body. I tried to discourage her. The way I understood it, the section of the river where Lucrecia took her life was not an open place, but a rushing stream cutting through a tangle of woodland, accessible only by a one-way, single lane, dirt road, full of ruts with few places to turn off. The road was known to university students, hardly a place where anyone would want to be found, or seen. Those too cheap or too shy to rent a motel room frequented it at night.

"Turning off River Road onto the dirt track through the woods, Susan hesitated, then she continued bumping along until she came to a clearing where there was room for several cars and she could see a section of the river dammed to make a swimming hole. Beside an old tree gripping the earth with huge roots partly submerged, two curly haired little boys fished with cane poles. She parked and walked over to where they sat on a rocky ledge."

'Hey, y'all. How's the fishin'?'

'Hey. It's good, M'am.' They scarcely glanced at her.

'What ya' catchin'?'

'Bluegill.'

'What ya' using for bait?'

'Bread dough.'

'That's good. Rolled up and mashed on the hook?'

'Yep. Works great.'

'How you boys get here?'

'Hiked.'

'You ever been here b'for'?'

'First time for me. Andy's been here once. He showed me the path.'

'You boys know anything about a college student who died somewhere around here a couple days ago? Seen any police?'

'"Naw. How'd she die?' The children glanced anxiously at each other.

'"Pills. She swallowed pills." The boys relaxed a little.

'"You boys be careful 'bout snakes, now. Y'hear? Watch where you put those bare feet. Snakes like to go fishin' too.' Susan turned and started back to her car.

"A frightened yelp twisted her around in time to see one of the boys drop a stringer of fish with a long wiggly form attached. The moccasin had more than half of the last fish down its throat.

"'Snake! Snake! Water moccasin! Run!'

"'What?'

"'Eating our fish! It swallowed the whole fish! Run!' The boys darted around her and disappeared along a path through a leafy tangle of low branches.

"The snake must have been attracted to the live fish on the stringer that the boys had attached to a root of the tree and hung in the water. Automatically, Susan went to her trunk and collected her hook and basket. Snatches of the old prayer chant ran through her mind. From the back seat, she took along a notebook and pen to write something for Lucrecia.

"The boys had abandoned their simple gear, poles rested where they'd been dropped. Carefully she pulled up the stringer. The snake was gone, the fish dead. They were small fish, about four to five inches by three and a half. After that, she didn't remember what she did or how much time passed, but a great calmness came over her.

"She remembered sitting on a flat stone among the tree roots and watching the dragonflies hover over the surface of the backwater, dragonflies so large she could hear their wings ripping the air. A vivid blue one came to her. She extended her hand. It darted away, then back to her finger tip where it rested, facing her, studying her with its huge compound eyes. She watched it hover, then zoom to her basket and land on the fastener holding the lid securely in place.

"A car jostled to a stop behind hers. Reality bumped roughly back with it. The spirit of the place shattered. A thunderhead blotted out the sunbeams playing in the foliage, and she saw Dr. Jestin step from the car. Instinctively, she grabbed the long handle of the snake hook and held it in both hands, angled across her body. The leer on his face disgusted her. She saw his lips moving, but she heard only some of his words, disassociated. Her determined, hardened expression probably gave him pause.

"He stopped coming toward her, looked at the basket and picked it up, still talking, still smiling at her.

"'. . . packed a lunch, how nice,' she heard him say. Watching her, he unfastened the lid and put his hand inside. His head snapped back in horror, his mouth and chest heaving with screams. The basket fell to the ground, but the long, chunky snake had wrapped itself around his wrist and stayed with him, fangs implanted.

"He grabbed the snake's body, pulling it from his wrist, but the snake released its bite, and the cottonmouth flashed again, striking his face. Jestin struggled, back tracking to rid himself of the entangling creature. His cries were so piercing, so pathetic, she half considered helping him. Flesh from his cheek tore away. He went down hard.

"She heard that sound, the sound of a skull cracking. The sound and the silence, then she heard the quiet movement of the moccasin gliding over the stones and through the roots at her feet to the water while she watched. It was the first time she ever deliberately let one go.

"She dropped the hook, picked up her notebook and went over the professor's body. She didn't feel for a pulse. There probably wouldn't be one. She was sure he'd cracked his head. A vein trailed black up his wrist from the snake bite. Blood flowed from the darkening wound on his face, more blood coursed from under his head, looking like night crawlers among sharp rocks, to a spot of orange-red dirt where it pooled and slowly sank in.

"Susan collected his blood on her finger and smeared 'No Picnic' across the open page. She closed the notebook, picked up her hook and basket and left without looking at him again. She knew he might not be dead, but he probably was, with two bites and a broken head. Rain in huge drops pelted the path like bombs. Lightening flashed, then the thunder rattled, indicating its proximity.

"No witness noticed her returning along River Road, nor did anyone question Dr. Jestin's death, although his place of death increased speculation about his connection with Lucrecia's suicide. There is, however, a ghost story which continues to the present, embellished over the years.

"Tell it, then," says Henrietta.

"During the questioning of the two youngsters whose poles they found, the police showed the boys a picture of Lucrecia.

"'It's her!' The boys swore she was the girl who told them she had died by taking pills. She'd warned them to watch out for snakes. No, they didn't remember any car or bicycle. She'd simply appeared. Although the ghost had saved their lives, neither thought they would fish there again.

"Some people say the co-ed's ghost took the form of a snake and killed her tormentor when he visited the place she died.

"Who's to say they're wrong about a ghost? The dragonfly recognized it.

"We never figured out how Jestin knew she had gone to the river. It must have been that silly, pale blue Falcon. Maybe he saw her driving toward River Road and guessed where she was going.

"When she returned to her dorm, Susan found the house mother regarding her with withering suspicion. 'The police'll want to know if you have any information about that Barry girl,' said the freshman women's guardian with two casualities in a week on her record.

"'Her name's Lucrecia.'"

"'A pretty little thing. I'm sorry about it, but some people aren't ready for college. The police have a suicide note. Her roommate found it before her parents came and took her home. You tell me if you remember anything to do with this business.'

"Susan went up to her room, closed the door and checked the shoe box on her closet shelf. In place of the jar, she found another note.

Kill him for me.
L.

"Tears, hot tears and sobs for her friend overtook Susan for a few moments, but abruptly, she stopped, blew her nose and wiped her eyes. She went to the mirror and straightened her blouse collar and stared at herself.

"'I did, Lucrecia. Maybe it was an accident, but I did. He's gone.'"

10.

Henrietta shifts her body in the wicker chair and rearranges her feet on the footstool we share. "When you finish Miss Susan's story, you can tell me your own, Miss Vivian. You're sad, but I don't think it's all on account of your husband's dying."

A sip of ice water sticks in my throat. I sputter, then cough. "You hush, Henrietta! Don't say such a thing. How can you talk like that?" I blot my dress front to avoid her look. Even in the growing darkness, I feel her eyes, and her words cut into me.

"I'm to trust you with my secrets, but you aren't willing to trust me with yours?"

"My life isn't that interesting. Just a simple. . . a simple shadowbox life." Needles poke my eyes. Needles of pain. I take Henrietta's offered tissue, blow my nose and straighten up. "I'll finish telling you about Susan."

"Susan tonight, you tomorrow night," she says.

I rush to continue. "What I'll tell you next, I've pieced together from campus gossip, friends on the staff and from Susan.

"Dean Edith Scoggins replaced the University Dean of Women who unexpectedly retired and departed from the campus that summer. Dean Scoggins was hired quickly, without the usual search process. Her reputation and her recommendations were exceptional, even in those areas noted for hyperbole. She came from six years at a well known women's college and was eager to move to a large, co-educational university. She seemed the perfect fit.

"For its part, the University needed to have its administrative staff complete for the fall quarter when their largest freshman class in years was due to start arriving at the end of August, forty-one percent of them young women. If there were any lingering resentments against the University, from families of female students, hiring the new dean should help.

"At the special meeting to introduce her, most of the all male senior staff liked her instantly. Tight grey ringlets swept to the top of her head crowned a round, perky face, covered with smile lines. She was much shorter than the previous dean of women and rounder, bouncier. Never married, but an outrageous flirt, the new dean became a celebrity when stories of her first meeting with this group leaked beyond the large conference room on the second floor of the administration building.

"Standing after her formal introduction to the group, as "Edy," and the usual silly joke that she already was standing, Dean Scoggins nodded to those around the table and noticed the president still on his feet, expecting her not to speak.

"'I'd like to say a few words, if I may.' The disarming smile radiated up, all over President Fox.

"'Certainly.' But Fox continued to stand, indicating her remarks should be short.

"'You must sit down. Take the load off. Tall men in dark suits make me so nervous. Remind me of pallbearers.' With a hand on his arm she urged him to sit. A few eyebrows rose in bemused expressions. With astonishing speed the new dean disappeared, then reappeared above the heavy table top with hands full of a stack of handbooks and binders. She chatted brightly about the University, the town, the people, while she divided the material into three uneven piles and put a set of papers on her chair.

"'I've reviewed all your policies, student handbooks, disciplinary procedures, what have you. These apply to all students, these to women students specifically, and this one thin item is the faculty and staff handbook. The preponderance of regulation, as you can see, deals with female students.

Remember that they also must follow the rules for the student body in general.' She patted the student handbook.

"'However, I understand. I spent years and years as a Naval officer and dean of women before coming here. Believe me, I'm familiar with this type of thing. But, a university that wants to stay in the forefront, wants to be a leader rather than a backwater, must be ready to examine its attitudes, even those it has never bothered to take out and look at.' Another flash of her big smile didn't last long enough to permit interruption. 'I find it quaint that we are so over-protective of our female students.'

"Two chubby hands raised palms out came together on her cheeks, emphasizing her expansive good nature. She talked in that fast, southern way of dispersing information, rapid firing with soft sounds: 'Over the next twenty years -- Begin with higher expectations for all students -- Morally, academically we need -- Move toward a future -- Protection leads to enslavement -- The antithesis of quality and equality is --

"'Gentlemen, all of this may sound naive, given the unspoken epidemic of rape this campus has experienced over the last few years, twenty-three cases, incidentally, and almost another twenty-odd suspicious ones, that we know about. I've been apprised fully by the former dean and a number of staff members. Part of my plan of attack will be speaking to the freshmen women, and men, at their first dorm meetings. I will be addressing the interfraternity and panhellenic councils, the upper classmen dorms. This fall, I will be convening a task force from the student body, and faculty, to draft a universal code of conduct. It needn't be long. Also, I plan awareness and prevention seminars for students. We need to challenge the under-culture. The one that says 'no' means 'yes'.

'"We have training sessions scheduled first thing next month, for all campus support personnel, including housemothers. I welcome you to attend any of these meetings. The schedule is here.' She divided the sheaf of papers from her chair in two and sent papers around the table in both directions. Off guard, each man took one while she continued. 'Our president, Dr. Fox, has assured me that he takes crime against female students seriously. Gentlemen, that is my mandate: we are going to guarantee that no one on this campus, ever again, down plays rape.'

'"About time. Bravo.' The grizzled, long-tenured, Dean of the School of Journalism clapped his hands, stood, and addressed President Fox. 'It's courageous leadership, facing this thing and openly combatting it. I like your new Dean of Women.'

"Dean Scoggins sent him a wink.

"Fox maintained a benign expression throughout it all, but his eyes had gone flat. No one challenged her, although most of the men must have felt she had overstepped. It was an era of politeness. She was so charming, bubbly. She sounded like

105

someone's grandmother giving a lesson in decorum. Milk and cookies would follow. Maybe one didn't have to take her seriously.

"Two nearly invisible secretaries in the room sat straighter. The President's personal secretary looked down to keep anyone from seeing her pleased expression. The other, also from the President's office, fumbled after her pen, dropped on the floor.

"'Interesting woman,' remarked the Agriculture department chairman to the head of Political Science, going down the steps.

"'Yeah, a real kick in the pants.' The men laughed, but the grumpy English department chairman, right behind them, maintained his funk.

"The Athletic Director said, 'I suppose we have to have a dean of women, but she's going to take over the staff meetings. We'll have to find a way to meet without her.'

"The waifish head of Fine Arts patted him on the back. 'It'll be fun watching our leader get bitter medicine from one of his own appointees. He has to stand by her. He's never admitted a mistake.'

"The room had cleared, and Dean Scoggins found herself with the two secretaries. One handed a note to the other and hurried off.

"'This is for you, Miss Scoggins.'

"The Dean took the note, read it with an 'Ah, ha' while the other secretary watched urgently.

"'I'd like to transfer to your office, Miss Scoggins. I'm a great typist and take very good shorthand.

"The new dean chuckled. 'That's the same request I have in this note. I thank you. Thank you both, but I am going to need friends in this office. I'm going to need all the friends I can get, long term, forever friends.'

"'You'll have them, I assure you.'

"And the word went out."

On the back porch the next afternoon, I hand Henrietta my copy of Death at Big Muddy.

"Read it," she says.

"Reread the passage I marked. Tell me who she's writing about."

Henrietta looks like she is headed into a trap. She reads in silence, more slowly than usual. This is the passage:

Most people would say the alligator is king of the swamp, but he's not. An old swamper friend told me the truth of it, so I know.

The old swamper followed the watery gator trails to his favorite fishing place, deep in the

Okefenokee. One particular day, he stopped and watched a bull alligator lazily dozing in open water. The man had seen this big gator in the past -- quiet, immobile, not bothering a thing.

A black bear, pushing through the undergrowth, ambled toward the water and plunged straight in and began swimming across. Without a ripple, the gator sank.

Fascinated, the swamper waited. When the bear was half way across, it bellowed and went under. Churning water and splashes hinted at the violence. Off to the side, the man's canoe began bobbing up and down. After a few moments, the bear surfaced and continued swimming across, same pace as before. Amazed, the man dragged for the gator and pulled him up.

He brought the gator back to the river station. I saw it. Daddy and I saw it. People took pictures. That old gator had his underside clawed clean away.

So, that's how I know the bear is king of the swamp.

'Course, that king might have been a she-bear.

Henrietta closes the book, chin up, pointing at me and glares.

"Any woman who thinks like a snake would surely compare another woman to a dragon fly or to a bear. You ain't the bear, so I'd guess the dean was."

I grin. "I didn't quite finish with the dean last night."

"You're not choosing to answer directly, so I guess I'm right then."

"Dean Scoggins brought Susan Ladona back to campus that fall. No one else could have done it. The new dean began at the infirmary, interviewed everyone privately, and found Red. Perhaps there were others, too, but through Red, the dean found Susan and talked her into returning.

"'I know what happened to you and I can guess the reason your friend, Lucrecia, killed herself. If you don't come back, this thing will haunt you all your life, cripple you,' the dean said.

"'You're wrong. I've all ready faced -- it.'

"'Prove it. Prove you're strong enough. Prove you have the courage to enjoy life, and study writing again. Prove it to me.'

"Susan only missed the freshmen orientation, the week before classes. On the dean's recommendation, she changed her major from English to journalism. Her first quarter she worked part-time in the dean's office so Edith Scoggins could monitor her progress and reassure Susan and her father, who knew only that she'd a bad experience with a recently deceased professor.

Her father didn't press for details and Susan gave none, both pretending the incident was trivial.

"The dean blocked the campus retaliatory processes, too, by making heroes of those who joined her campaign against rape. The student newspaper led with the story in its first issue. The newspaper in town picked it up and followed with in-depth interviews of experts and a 'myths versus reality' feature. Reporters from papers in other cities and the state capital called. The governor's wife visited campus and singled out Dean Scoggins for special phrase. The unreconstructed individuals on campus began to keep their views to themselves."

11.

A big cockroach somehow made it through the screening and flew to the wicker end table near my lemonade and Henrietta's tea. I folded a section of newspaper and swung the same instant Henrietta snatched away the glasses. It took five good swats to squash the insect on the rough surface. I would have given it more, but Henrietta told me I could quit. She looked at the creature's bashed body, wings splayed, goo oozing into the wicker. "I think it's dead, Miz Vivian." She exaggerated her accent, as if I were Nurse Martha. Henrietta replaced the glasses, whipped away the liquid that had sloshed onto her hands then used the napkin to pick up the roach remains. "Guess you're not like your friend Susan."

"Sorry for the mess. They trigger a reaction in me."

"I see that. Still it's one of nature's creatures."

"Henrietta, you don't like bugs either."

"Not in the house or near the food, but you are something else." She gave me her big eyes look. "Should I get the 409 and a sponge for you to finish cleaning up the table?"

"Ah --, yes, please." So, we're partners. Partners in the clean up of roach guts.

That evening we chatted about the price of produce, menus for the next few days, nothing else relating to Susan. When we went inside for the night, Henrietta said, "Tomorrow evening is your turn."

In the morning Henrietta made sticky buns, my favorite, for breakfast. I eat three, but I'm in no mood to be pacified. She's pushing, and I don't like it. We don't talk much over breakfast. "It's going to be a scorcher," I say. She grunts agreement. "Worse than yesterday," I say. She nods and clears the dishes.

She sees me to the porch where I'll read until the heat forces me to go to the back proch or inside and sit in front of a fan. She surprises me and sits down too, in the rocker.

"Thought you had ironing to do." The words sound cross, and I feel ashamed.

"Too hot for ironing. Things can wait a spell. I'll just keep you company fo' a while."

"I thought you liked to get the work done early while it's cool." I hear my desperation. Henrietta has probably heard it too.

112

She's rocking, ever so slightly, just rocking and humming, saying nothing.

Finally she says, "Some times a burden is lighter when it's shared."

I sag in my chair and look at the sky through the pink-fringed blossoms of the mimosa tree out front. The tree with the lacy leaves that close protectively when touched.

"Oh, you're right, Henrietta. I feel a little sad about my husband but it's out of understanding and pity, not love." There's an edge in my voice. It comes from deep inside, from a place I thought I'd buried it forever, under pleasantries, and politeness and smiles.

"After our first anniversary, my marriage was nothing but a business arrangement. There was no sex, not after our first fourteen months together. We did become friends, over the years.

"My dad had made it very clear to me that I could never come home. Not that he and mother disapproved of my husband; they were thrilled with him and delighted that I had married such wealth and prestige. Dad believed allowing women to return home at the first sign of a problem was the cause of many divorces. And, believe me, neither family approved of divorce.

"I did talk to a friend, early on, but my mother-in-law heard about it and -- . Well, I never talked to anyone after that.

113

"Susan knew. She guessed. She wrote that my letters sang with joy when I wrote about my third graders, but were mechanical otherwise. I never expressed any regret about not having children, she told me. But I do regret it. 'You love your work,' She wrote. 'Teaching has become your whole life. Is it enough?'

"I scribbled 'It has to be' on a postcard and didn't write again for a while.

"My father-in-law once told me that my husband had picked me for my looks and sense of style. He acted like it was a compliment. He didn't disagree when I jokingly compared his comments to a horse auction, though.

"My husband never stopped paying attention to other women. He saw more bedrooms than a chamber maid at one of the downtown hotels.

"I'd loved him once, I think. Thought he loved me. Funny, huh? But when I got over the sentimentality, I surprised myself.

"We negotiated a contract. For playing the role of the loving wife, I could have a bank account in my own name. Back then, a woman couldn't even open a bank account without her husband's permission."

"Or your employer's," Henrietta says.

"Yes, you know what it was like. At least my teaching salary was my own. He agreed to my requests. I agreed to give no hint, no cough, roll of an eye, not a word, that we were anything but a happy couple. I became an actress in a never ending play.

"It was easier and easier to live a lie. I had my teaching. I volunteered at the hospital when school was out. Couldn't join him on many business trips that way. Twenty-five years slipped by." I breathe in the morning air, already heavy. My lungs feel like they aren't getting enough oxygen.

"Two years ago, I became involved with a doctor who worked in research at the Centers for Disease Control. We planned to marry." My words tumble out, trying to get ahead of the tears. "My husband, Cody, knew. We'd even talked about a quiet divorce and maybe staying connected as friends. That was before the --. There -- there was an accident at the lab. Tucker contaminated himself with some horrible ten-minute bacteria, Ebola -- not Ebola. It's a virus, but something weird like that. It ate his flesh." I squeeze my burning eyes shut and pinch off the flood draining from my nose. My mouth gulps for air. "There was one quick call to say good-bye, while he was still isolated in the lab. They wouldn't let me see him. I couldn't speak to him after that. He was gone in three days."

Henrietta has stopped rocking. Her eyes watch me. Her head nods.

I wipe my dripping nose with the back of my hand, then my sleeve. "Cody's crash was less than a week later. So here I am trying to sort out my life and feeling sorry for myself." I hear nervous laughter, and realize it's my own.

Henrietta rises to her feet using both hands on the arms of the rocker as she always does. She puts the box of tissues in my lap and pats my shoulder as she passes me on her way to the door. "After you finish your strengthening exercises, you'll go right over to the school. They need you to help out in those summer classes. You hear me, Miss Vivian? No sass now."

12.

I'm thinking about that conversation with Henrietta, one week ago, and how thankful I am for the push she gave me when the telephone interrupts. It's Susan.

"You're not easy to find," she says after we exchange greetings. "I had to try information twice. Did you get my new book? What do you think?"

"It . . . Well, it wasn't what I expected. Actually, I was shocked, if you must know. It's -- different. Not what happened. Not what you told me."

"Vivian -- "

"It's, it's so romanticized."

"You're angry. Disappointed. But Viv, I have no anger. I let go of it long ago. It would have strangled me."

"You wrote of a seduction, a cruel seduction granted, but still--"

"Think about it, Viv. It's not that much of a stretch. Dr. Jestin was good looking, knowledgeable. Naiveté played a part but maybe not as big a part as I wanted to believe. I was foolish to go out to his house. Stupid. Maybe intrigued. Maybe the warning voices sang a tantalizing song.

"He was a sexual predator! You didn't deserve --"

"Stupidity has a high price, Viv. Yes, he was a sexual predator, but he did teach students something about literature and writing."

"Why are you defending him?"

"I'm not! I just tried to see him as he might have seen himself. The character needed his own voice. In giving him one, he became someone else. The story changed. The characters take charge. It's not my story or Jestin's any more, but something else." She paused. "Viv, why are you still hanging on to this anger? All these years?"

Her question hits me in the stomach. I can't answer.

"Don't tell me it's because of some sense of loyalty to me. If I let it go, you must."

I can barely hear my own response. "You're right. Who knows? If I'd realized you were over it, I wouldn't have -- "

"Viv, the reason I called is to tell you something else. Something I think only you will understand."

"Something else? What?"

"Several days ago I was writing in my study when the telephone roused me with its queer burst of noise. My hands wavered over the computer keys then moved to rub the back of my neck. I went into the next room to answer it. I never do that. Never when I'm writing.

"Sis! How are you? I forgot to turn off the ringer, or I wouldn't have answered. The air conditioning's on the fritz. I'm drowning in sweat. New York's just like being in the swamp. What's up?"

"Sue, it's important or I wouldn't have called in the morning.

"Unk's gone. Died yesterday afternoon. I couldn't reach you. Didn't want to leave that kind of message."

"Thanks, Sis. It's sad, but his suffering's over."

"Yeah. There's one more thing. Dad opened his copy of the will. The lawyer will be notifying us officially, but I thought you might like to know."

"Know what?"

"Well, Unk left most of his assets to Daddy, with some cash for his crew, the way he said he would. He left me the alligator farm, the land and buildings, that is. Pretty valuable piece of property."

"That's great."

"Sue?"

"Yes."

"It's so strange. He left you all the gators and snakes. -- Sue?"

"Oh! Unk. He did it. He really did it! That's great."

"Great? Sue? I don't understand."

"Yes, it's perfect."

As she relates this conversation, I imagine how Susan took the news. The smile starting small and widening across the china doll face. Diamonds flashing in the earth and sky eyes. A pearl tear escaping. One, then another, from each eye.

"I can see your face, Susan. You haven't stopped glowing, I'll bet." I laugh. "I mean I'm sorry about your uncle, but you have your sign."

"Yes, I knew there're be a sign."

13.

The rusty spring screeches in protest. The back door opens and slaps shut after Henrietta steps inside. I gather my school work spread out on the kitchen table and hurry to pour an iced tea for her. Sweat's pouring from her face, but she insists on her walks.

Henrietta has returned from marketing with fresh peaches and salad greens and big, locally grown tomatoes. She knows I enjoy fresh fruits and vegetables. We put some of the things away and then sit for a while so she can catch her breath.

She eyes me. "What you so giddy about? Looks like you're about to burst.

My reserve vanishes. "I have news." My too-wide smile gives me away. Henrietta waits, suspicious of surprises. "I interview for a permanent position tomorrow. Third grade teacher's husband was transferred.

Henrietta smiles. With her lips, not her teeth, but it's a real smile that lights her whole face. "Still going to be wanting full-time help around here?"

"Of course! There's nothing busier than a third grade teacher. Anyway, there's more."

"And what's that?" Henrietta rises, brings a knife and plate to the table, sits and starts to peel a peach for herself.

"Will you make a peach pie for the week-end?" I ask.

Her chin points up at me. "What fo'?" she asks. "We just finished one. How about rhubarb?"

"Susan Ladona called this morning. She's in Atlanta, on her way back to New York. Been down in Florida. She'll be visiting on Saturday. I told her that she should meet you, hear your story. What you told me."

Henrietta's chin juts further. Her eyes narrow. I keep talking and work with long-stemmed sunflowers at the sink.

"She has her tenth book started, but your story might be the germ of something for the one after that. She wants to meet you."

Henrietta stares at me. A hint of interest. Not the blank look she's perfected. She stops slicing the peach and points the paring knife at me. I grin at the threat.

"I also told her you made a wicked peach pie."

I'm still giggling about this as I take the flowers into the living room. Afraid I didn't dry the bottom of the vase, Henrietta is right behind me with a dish towel. Out front, in the heat, a man wearing a dark suit and tie and a woman in a suit and white, frilly-necked blouse are stepping from a car, grey, with some kind of a seal on it. Henrietta stares, from them to me. She swings around toward the kitchen. I'm right behind her. "Who are they, Henrietta? You know them?"

She looks away, sighs, sinks into a kitchen chair and runs her fingers over the scar on her face. The bell rings.

"Miss Vivian . . . Vivian, I, I applied for a job."

"Jeez, Henrietta! Why not just ask for a raise? I'd have -- "

Her hands go up, palms out. "A different job. Completely different. I gave you as a reference."

I frown, ignore the plea in her voice. "I thought you liked it here. Working for me." I can't keep the stinging anger out of my voice. The bell rings again. "When were you going to tell me?"

Her hands come together, eyes close a moment, open and look into mine.

"It's something I want very much. I want it, Vivian."

The bell again, held down this time. Closing the kitchen door behind me, I hurry to answer.

"Why, hello. You must forgive me. I was busy in the kitchen. How can I help you?"

"I'm Mr. Bradishaw with the University Personnel and this is Mrs. McQuarter, Dean of the School of Living Skills. We'd like

123

to talk to you about Henrietta Elmers. She works for you, doesn't she?"

"Oh, my, yes! Henrietta is wonderful. Do come in and sit down. You must be dying in this heat. I'll get you some iced tea."

I dash to the kitchen, close the door and whisper to Henrietta, "They're from the University."

"I applied for a teaching position."

"A teaching position?"

"Cooking. Teaching cooking."

"Teaching cooking -- at the University." I mop up the tea I've spilled on the counter, drop a lemon wedge in each glass, push open the door and head back to the living room. I compliment Mrs. McQuarter on her Laurel Burch cat pin and ear rings.

Mr. Bradishaw says he guesses that Mrs. Elmers has told me her intentions to join the staff.

"Oh, yes. We were discussing it very recently."

Mrs. McQuarter said, "We have a few questions. Won't take too much of your time." She sips. I distribute little linen napkins and over my guests' heads, see the kitchen door quietly close to a crack.

"Have you actually known Henrietta for nearly thirty years? All that time?" Mrs. McQuarter asks.

I smile, cultivate soft consonants, look directly at my guests. "She ran the campus residence where I lived at the College of William and Mary in Virginia."

"I thought she was the cook." Mrs. McQuarter is fingering her pin.

"The best cook on campus, without question, but she also managed a large portion of the budget and influenced the manners and demeanor of us all." My guests smile. "Since you've met Henrietta, you realize how quickly she exerts her organizing skills. All to the good, I must say."

"Yes, m'am." Mr. Bradishaw laughs. "We suspected that."

"How's her health?" asks Mr. Bradishaw.

"Healthy as a horse."

Mrs. McQuarter coughs. "She's honest, of course."

"Completely."

"You recommend her without any reservation whatsoever? Guardian of morality and all that?"

"Without equivocation, I can state that Henrietta will go to extreme lengths to protect children and young people." I pause, then say, "Raised three children alone. They're all professionals. I believe you know her son? At the University. Dr. Elmers. In agronomy."

"Yes, indeed we do. Very quiet, well-mannered, seems to be a fine teacher." Mrs. McQuarter gives me the impression they've talked to him.

"Henrietta seems to be a remarkable woman," Mr. Bradishaw says, "largely self-educated, talented. We have only a few follow-up questions to her application."

"What about integrity? What's her weak point?" Mrs. McQuarter asks.

"Not everyone understands her sense of humor. But that's their shortcoming, not hers. As to integrity. Her integrity is every bit as good as my own. Better, maybe." I hold the woman's eyes with mine. "I know of nothing she has done that you would question. Nothing I've ever questioned." I use a powdered sugar expression. They finish their tea. Mr. Bradishaw centers his glass on the damp napkin.

"What happened to her husband?" he asks.

A quick scraping sound escapes from behind the kitchen door.

"Cat's hungry I guess. I've had a busy morning," I say.

"Oh," says Mrs. McQuarter, glancing around at the floor.

"We wondered what happened to her husband." Mr. Bradishaw doesn't seem to have the same feeling for cats.

"She had two husbands. I know that. Both long dead."

"Ever divorced?" asks Mrs. McQuarter.

"Widowed twice. When she was young.

Doesn't the University have a policy on such personal questions, though? I was simply wondering. Kind of a personal question."

I have done my best to couch the threat in the colloquial style. In California I would have said, nicely, "I don't believe you may ask that, legally."

Mrs. McQuarter blushes and rises to leave. I rise too, step to the door. "Anyway, you are going way back. Henrietta'd lost both husbands before I met her." I see them off with "She has my highest recommendation!"

Linda Lanterman

14.

"Why'd you lie?"

"Because I'm good at it!" Feelings of betrayal resurface but not fiercely.

Henrietta, face blank, watches me. "Thought you gave up lying."

"Little back-sliding."

Her face softens. She turns to the sink so I won't see her, but there's a laugh in her voice and she shakes her head. "Girl, you're hopeless."

Henrietta's name is Helen in Susan's novel <u>A Drowning in Flowery Branch</u>. I didn't recognize much of Henrietta's story beyond her physical description and gestures, but when I got past that, I enjoyed reading the novel. Susan still uses green ink for her notes. She dedicated this one to Henrietta and sent her the first copy.

Henrietta calls me Sister Vivian or just Sister these days. She didn't work for me long. The University recruited her to teach Traditional Southern Cooking, a course in the Living Skills department. That was home economics in my day. Adjunct Professor they call her. She's also team teaching a course in institutional food management for the Center for Continuing Education. It's a "distance learning" course televised throughout the state at 6 to 7 am and 5 to 6 pm on the University's channel. I started out watching it religiously, but it made me miss her too much. I tape it now, or watch snatches. She's like a different person, happy. Her insights, her body language, even her "uh-huhs" translate well on camera. Friends ask me about her, tell me how much they like her show.

She leased her old house and moved closer to the University. Forty-seven miles away. We planned to get together every other week, halfway in between, but Henrietta doesn't drive at night any more. And, ever since I served her fish tacos and salad greens with fresh mango and papaya chunks, she hasn't made it back. Says there's no one to drive her down to my place. I don't think she shares my enthusiasm for California cuisine.

I go up for an afternoon and evening every month or two. We eat out mostly. Sometimes we talk about teaching methods and cognitive development and learning theory. She tells me about the challenges of teaching college students and working in front of a camera. Once in a while we go to a movie, but best of all, are the times we sit on her porch and trade stories, happier stories now. And we laugh.

#